Furniture Repair & Refinishing

Jeff Jewitt

Handyman Club Library™

Handyman Club of America
Minnetonka, Minnesota

Furniture Repair & Refinishing

By Jeff Jewitt

CREDITS

Tom Carpenter
Creative Director

Mark Johanson
Book Products Development Manager, Editor, Contributing Writer

Dan Cary
Photo Production Coordinator, Technical Editor & Content Supervisor

Jeff Jewitt
Author

Bill Nelson
Series Design, Art Direction and Production

Mark Macemon
Lead Photographer

Ralph Karlen
Photography

Brad Classon, John Nadeau, Randy Wackerfuss
Production Assistance

SPECIAL THANKS

Old Science Renovation, Inc., of Minneapolis, Minnesota and staff:
Terry Lee Storhaug, Heather Jacbos, Don Sellers, Sam Sellers, Woody Smith, Mike Hardy, Pat Landis, Randy Wackerfuss

Lee Waldon, Waldon Woods Antiques, Minneapolis, Minnesota

ISBN 10: 1-58159-142-X
ISBN 13: 978-1-58159-142-2
© 2001 Handyman Club of America
6 7 8 9 10 / 15 14 13 12 11 10

Handyman Club of America
12301 Whitewater Drive
Minnetonka, Minnesota 55343
www.handymanclub.com

Furniture Repair & Refinishing

Table of Contents

Introduction

In my younger days, I acquired what would be my first furniture restoration project: a walnut dresser that I rescued from my parents' basement. This poor chest of drawers was not in great condition, and back then I didn't even know that walnut was a premium wood. The finish had darkened to a dreary black, the drawers barely operated, the back panel was falling off and the whole frame was loose. Nonetheless, the old dresser was the right price, and it followed me from apartment to apartment and finally to the garage of my very first house, where it remained, banished to a life of holding bicycle parts and sports equipment, until eventually I decided to fix it.

First, I reglued all the drawers so the sides didn't fall apart when you pulled the drawers open. Then I removed the top, disassembled the frame joints as far as I could, and glued everything back together. I stripped the old, dark finish and replaced it with two coats of varnish. I even crafted a new decorative wooden escutcheon. To this day, I remember how proud I was of what I had done. I had given new life to the old wreck, and when the sun glanced across the revived walnut surface in the early evening, the wood looked as beautiful as any I had ever seen.

The satisfaction and pride I felt after that first restoration has led me into a lifelong career of restoring and refinishing furniture. I still tingle a bit when I bring a customer's piece of furniture back to its former glory. I suspect most other folks feel the same way when they restore a cherished family heirloom of their own.

Furniture Repair & Refinishing is produced by and for the Members of the Handyman Club of America. It is about everything I've learned since I first tackled that old walnut dresser in my garage so long ago. While we tend to think of antiques or very old furniture when we talk about repairing and restoring furniture, modern furniture needs attention and repairs almost as much as older furniture. So this book will deal with repairs first, dealing with broken and missing parts, loose frames and such. In the second section we'll get into the more involved tasks of stripping and restoration. Whatever your skill level you should find plenty of information and advice on simple repairs, as well as complex ones. In the end, I only hope that you feel that same warm satisfaction I still get when I see furniture destined for the garage sitting proudly and grandly in someone's living or dining room.

It's important to understand the dynamics of why wood furniture gets loose, splits, cracks or basically just starts falling apart. The basic question becomes: "If it's well made to begin with, why doesn't it stay that way?"

As a material, wood is plentiful, surprisingly strong for its weight, and it can be easily cut, shaped and finished in ways no other material can. It has one essential quality, though, that poses a problem: wood likes water. Wood is hydroscopic, meaning it will take moisture out of the air when the air is moist, and it will release it when the air is dry. This causes the wood to shrink and swell, changing its physical dimensions ever so slightly as the surrounding environment changes. This constant expansion/contraction is what eventually causes many tight-fitting joints to loosen or break over time. This, in conjunction with the ongoing stress of normal use, contributes to the number one problem to afflict wood furniture—it gets loose. Other factors add in as well. Sunlight, air, heat and moisture all cause finishes to crack and turn yellow. Stains fade and, in extreme cases, cause the wood to crack and split. Feisty two-year-olds, puppies and moving companies can exact other stress-related tolls as well.

Repairs to wood furniture fall into three general categories: regluing, replacing wood and repairing the finish. Regluing is the most common furniture repair, regardless of the age of the furniture. We'll take a look at the types of glues that are best suited for regluing, as well as the best regluing techniques. Wood that's split, broken or missing will be discussed next, followed by repairs to the surface and finish.

~JJ

IMPORTANT NOTICE

For your safety, caution and good judgment should be used when following instructions described in this book. Take into consideration your level of skill and the safety precautions related to the tools and materials shown. Neither the publisher, North American Membership Group, Inc., nor any of its affiliates can assume responsibility for any damage to property or persons as a result of the misuse of the information provided. Consult your local building department for information on permits, codes, regulations and laws that may apply to your project.

AFTER

BEFORE

Is it worth it? *That's the basic question you need to ask yourself before leaping into a difficult restoration project. There's no way to know for sure, of course, but it's good to know that sometimes (as you can see here) the answer is an emphatic "Yes!"*

Evaluating Furniture Restoration Projects

There are really very few pieces of furniture in most homes that wouldn't benefit from some attention. A scratch that needs filling, a loose rung that needs tightening, a finish that could use some touching up. But when does a routine maintenance project cross the line to become a major repair and refinishing project? And, more importantly, when should it?

Like many things in life, deciding whether or not to embark on a major furniture restoration project is essentially a matter of weighing cost against benefit. "How much will it cost?" and "How long will it take?", versus "How much do I stand to gain?" To answer these questions requires careful evaluation. If you examine the furniture piece closely, it will probably provide the answer. The "Before" shots of furniture on the following pages are intended to point out a few of the questions you'll want to ask as part of your own furniture evaluation.

While the whole cost/benefit approach makes sense if you're evaluating a potential furniture purchase

(especially with an eye toward making a profit on it), it is of little use when it comes to furniture you already own. Particularly, furniture that has sentimental value. Ask most professional refinishers and they will probably confess to one fact: many of the estimates they give for a full restoration are in excess of the value of the piece—even after the work is done. But people do it anyway, because, to them, it's worth it. Furniture holds memories of people and important times in our lives. It becomes not just an old trunk, but a family heirloom. And we'll go to a lot of effort and expense to fix it—not so much because we want it for ourselves, but because we want to pass it on. To someone special.

Whether you're doing it for the money or for the sake of preserving memories, you will need to know what's in store. Reading through the examples on the following pages will help. Also, throughout the book you'll find short features from "The Refinisher's File." These case studies of start-to-finish restoration projects will give you a nice taste of what you can expect.

How bad is the damage? *Wood breaks. But some types of damage are much easier to repair than others. The school desk above is on the easier-to-repair side because the large split is not at a natural stress point and none of the wood in the damaged area is missing. Watch out for furniture that is missing significant amounts of wood in high-stress areas, like joints.*

What is the condition of the finish? *A finish that looks like the one above leaves no doubt that you'll need to remove it completely. In some cases removing a finish is a snap, in others it's a nightmare. If you don't know what kind of finish you have, do some testing (See page 73) and find out. Then you'll have a better idea how much work will be involved in removing it.*

What is it made of? *This can be a more difficult question to answer than you might think. If you know the piece is made of hardwood, especially one of the more desirable species, the project stands a good chance for success. The cute mantel clock to the right looked like a good potential project until we dabbed off a bit of finish and discovered what it was actually made of: cardboard.*

Do I have the skills to fix it? *None of the repair and refinishing help this stool needs requires advanced woodworking skills, but if you're unwilling to or unable to do any upholstery work, it wouldn't be worth starting the project.*

What is the best-case scenario? *This kids' rocker certainly has potential for improvement, but even if everything goes as planned, what is the most that can be expected of it? A cute, but very common, little chair of minimal monetary value? Or a cherished keepsake for someone you care about?*

What is the style? *Value and design style are quite interrelated. These days, if something is Mission style, as this plant stand is, it is almost certainly worth putting some time and expense into. The flip side of this coin, however, is that a poorly thought-out or even an overly aggressive restoration can greatly decrease the value of the object. If you even suspect you've got something collectible or valuable, consult a reputable antiques dealer before you do anything to it.*

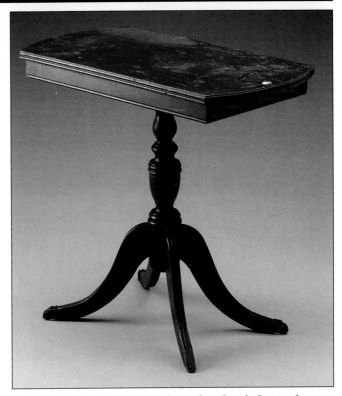

Will a limited restoration do the job? *Other than on the tabletop (where complete stripping and refinishing is obviously needed), the finish on this pedestal table is in pretty good shape, making it a good candidate for a limited restoration. In such a procedure, some or all of the finish is left in place, saving quite a bit of time and effort.*

What is it? *If you don't know, that may be a bad sign. But don't give up on it. Find out. Do some research and ask questions. You may find you have a whole new appreciation for the piece (the one shown here is an early 19th-century bucket bench, by the way).*

Are stains in the finish only? *Many kinds of stains that affect furniture can be cleaned up or removed. The biggest determining factor is whether the stain is in the finish layer only, or has penetrated the finish into the wood. On this chest, the black stains had made it into the wood but turned out to be bleachable.*

Repairing Furniture

Furniture can fail for many reasons and in many ways. When it does, you'll find there are equally numerous options for what to do about it. Perhaps the most common response is to do nothing. Loose joints or scratches in the surface are not, by themselves, serious enough problems to prompt most of us into action. But eventually, more serious problems will develop and the furnishing will become useless. When this happens, it's time to either get busy repairing or to part with the piece.

When you do them yourself, most furniture repairs are not difficult or expensive—just time consuming. Especially if you want to do the job correctly. Very often disassembly is involved in order to make strong new glue joints. You may have to create a new part or two. In this section you'll learn how to make all the most common furniture repairs the right way.

Good match with Colonial maple stick!

Tools & Materials

When it comes to repairing wood, you'll be pleased to learn how much you can do with a basic inventory of hand tools. Even when a special tool is called for, it's usually possible to improvise. Professionals are masters at improvising clever jigs and clamping devices, and finding new uses for basic tools. Of course, if you do have furnituremaking machinery, like a table saw, band saw, jointer or planer, it can speed up some tasks quite a bit. But even with a shopful of furnituremaking machinery, you may well find that hand tools generally are quicker and easier to use.

Hand tools

Most hand tools you're likely to need when repairing furniture can be found at just about any hardware store. But use some sound decision making whenever you purchase a new tool. There is no shortage of cheap or gimmicky tools in the retail market. Resist the temptation to opt for the lowest-priced tool on the shelf, and avoid the prepackaged, no-name sets.

Before purchasing any tool, pick it up and hold it to see how it feels in your hand. And use some discretion at auctions and flea markets. While there are always "bargains" to be had, many old tools will need a lot of cleaning and tweaking to work correctly, and the metal may be damaged or pitted badly from rusting.

Screwdrivers. When working on older furniture, you'll need an assortment of flathead, square-head and phillips-head screwdrivers. Look for tools with cushioned grips and shafts made from high quality steel. In addition, it's useful to keep an old mid-sized flathead in your tool kit that you can dress on a bench grinder to fit older screws precisely. You should have at least three phillips-head screwdrivers (small, medium and large). On newer furniture you'll likely run into square-head or even torx-head screws that will totally exasperate you unless you have screwdrivers made to fit these head shapes. A cordless drill/driver with a full complement of driver bits can be very helpful. While practically useless for flathead screws, they're first-rate for driving or removing phillips-head and square-head screws. When it comes to delicate screws, though, hand-powered screwdrivers provide greater control than drill/drivers.

Hand saws. There are two choices here, *Western* style or *Eastern* (Japanese) style. A mixture of the two styles is good. Western-style saws are better for bigger jobs, like rip-cutting and cross-cutting. *Rip saws* have fewer teeth per inch (TPI) for a more aggressive cut. Both a *back saw* and its smaller cousin, a *dovetail saw*, are indispensable for smaller, delicate work. In the Eastern camp, the Japanese *dozuki* is terrific for very fine, controlled cutting. A flexible, *Japanese flush-cutting saw* is the best tool for cutting off dowels and plugs flush to the wood surface. Because Japanese saws cut on the pull stroke, they take a bit of getting used to. But they have thinner, highly tempered blades, resulting in saws that cut more finely and stay sharper longer. Specialized saws include a *coping saw* for making scrolled or curved cuts, and a *veneer saw* for cutting veneer. A *hacksaw* is absolutely necessary if you have to cut metal.

Hammers. You'll need several of these. *Claw hammers* are used both to drive and to remove nails. Buy one that feels comfortable in your hand. Generally, lighter hammers (16 ounces) offer better control than heavier framing hammers (22 ounces). A *rubber-head mallet* is good for knocking apart furniture joints. A *dead-blow mallet* weighted with shot inside the head works great for this purpose. Also handy is a wood or hard-rubber *striking mallet* for driving wood chisels. Using a metal hammer to strike a wooden chisel can damage the chisel.

Screwdrivers are essential for furniture repair. A good set includes small, medium and large flathead and phillips tools, an old flathead screwdriver that can be ground to fit troublesome screws, a square-drive model, jeweler's screwdrivers for fine work and a drill/driver bit with assorted tips.

Hand saws handy for furniture work include: (A) rip saw; (B) cross-cut saw; (C) hacksaw; (D) coping saw; (E) veneer saw; (F) dovetail saw; (G) Japanese flush-cutting saw; (H) Japanese dozuki saw; (I) back saw.

Hammers and mallets useful for furniture repair include: (A) a rubber-head mallet; (B) a 16-ounce claw hammer; (C) a dead-blow mallet for knocking apart joints; (D) a tack hammer for driving brads and tacks; (E) a wood-head mallet.

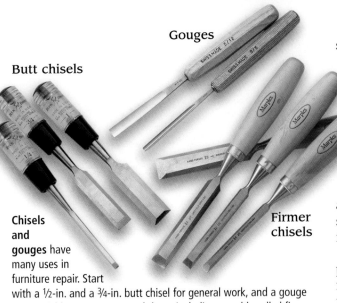

Gouges

Butt chisels

Firmer chisels

Chisels and gouges have many uses in furniture repair. Start with a ½-in. and a ¾-in. butt chisel for general work, and a gouge or two. Add more as you need them, including wood-handled firmer chisels for carving work.

Planes, rasps, files and scrapers are used for making replacement parts, general wood repairs, surface preparation and even removing old finishes. Tools shown above are : (A) jack plane; (B) spokeshave; (C) cabinet scraper; (D) riffler; (E) combination rasp; (F) wood file; (G) single-cut metal file; (H) block plane; (I) rabbet plane.

Painter's tools are used mainly for removing old finishes. You'll need both a large and small putty knife. A palette knife is used for removing finish in delicate areas and for applying putties. A 5-in-1 scraping tool can reach into just about any area.

Chisels. In furniture repair, you'll find uses for both square-end and curved chisels (called gouges). Square-end chisels come in different widths, from ⅛ to several inches, but for most work you can get by with a ½-in. and a ¾-in. A pair of straight gouges, which are measured by both width across the tool's cutting edge and the sweep or depth of the curve (a higher number means a deeper curve) will come in handy.

Look for *out-cannel* gouges, which can be identified by a sharpened bevel on the outside of the blade. Get a ½-in. gouge with low (number 5 or so) sweep and a smaller, ¼-in. tool with a number 9 sweep (indispensable for paring out dowel holes).

Scrapers, planes and rasps. If you don't have a power planer or joiner, bench planes are essential for furniture repair work. A *jack plane* or *smoothing plane* is used to reduce wood thickness to the final dimension (of the two, a jack plane is a little more versatile). A *block plane* is small enough to be operated with one hand, making it perfect for general trimming and for detail work, such as chamfering edges. A rabbet plane, like the Stanley 92, is very useful for trimming joints to fit. It can also be converted to a chisel plane for trimming up corners. *Hand scrapers* (also called *cabinet scrapers*) are used for delicate trimming and for removal of old glue. *Rasps* and *files* can shape convex and concave profiles, from a gentle curve to more complex forms. A large patternmaker's rasp is great for roughing out shapes quickly. Look for a smaller detail file for delicate shaping work. Double-duty tools feature four distinct surfaces: a half-round and a flat rasp on one end, and a half-round and a flat file on the other end. The smaller, tapered-end versions of these tools are better for detailing. Rasps have large teeth that remove wood quickly. A file makes a less aggressive cut for smoothing. In addition, a metal file like a single-cut, mill bastard is handy for smoothing metal.

Paint scrapers and putty knives. A paint scraper like the one pictured at left is a highly versatile multipurpose tool. Its hefty blade can be used for both scraping and prying. It also features several shaped scraping edges, including half-round, angled and straight. The stiff metal blade can be re-ground easily with a file or a bench grinder. Putty knives in different widths are used for applying putty. For more precise applications of wood putty, see if you can find a palette knife at your local art supply store.

Knives. Surprisingly, a plain old pocket knife gets about as much use as any other cutting tool in the professional furniture repair shop. A mat knife (for cutting picture-frame mats) and a craft knife (with spare blades) get a good workout as well. I prefer these two tools for cutting veneer, and the mat knife can be used for some trimming work. Both work as scribing tools for marking.

Vises. Ideally, you should have two vises mounted to

your primary worksurface: a *woodworking vise* that mounts underneath the bench for holding wood parts, and a *bench vise* with metal serrated jaws for holding metal and other items securely. Of the two, the bench vise has a bit more to offer for general use. If you have only a metal-jaw bench vise in your shop, make a pair of wooden jaw inserts to drop down over the serrated metal jaws when holding wood parts.

Sharpening stones. Since even the best cutting tools are ineffective if they're dull, you'll want a good sharpening stone to maintain the edges on your chisels and knives. There are two types of sharpening stones to choose from: *oilstones* and *water stones* (referring to the type of lubricant you use when applying a blade to the stone). A good general-purpose stone is a *combination oilstone,* with coarse grit on one face and fine-to-medium grit on the other. TIP: When sharpening with an oilstone, try using kerosene as the lubricant.

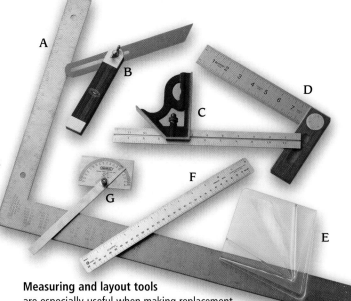

Measuring and layout tools
are especially useful when making replacement parts for broken furniture. Some of the most useful are: (A) carpenter's (framing) square; (B) sliding T-bevel; (C) combination square; (D) try-square; (E) center finder; (F) steel ruler; and (G) protractor.

Keep your blades and cutters sharp with a quality whetstone (a combination oilstone with both a coarse and a fine grit face is shown above).

Pliers. The three most essential types of pliers you'll need are *standard, side-cutting* and *needle-nose.* Though used less frequently, end nippers are handy for trimming small nails and brads, and they also make a great pulling and prying tool for nails and other fasteners (See page 23).

Measuring tools. A *tape measure* is the tool to use for taking larger measurements, but you won't find much use for one in furniture repair, where a 12-in. *metal rule* is the star of the show. A full-size *framing (carpenter's) square* is reliable when checking for squareness of drawers and cabinets. A *combination square* is well suited for intricate layout work. A *sliding T-bevel* and *adjustable protractor* are the basic tools you'll need for transferring odd angles.

Nailsets and marking tools. *Nailsets* are used to drive nailheads below the wood surface. *Countersinks* are used to cut a tapered entry hole for counter-sinking screws. Marking tools include a *scribe* or *scratch awl* for marking.

Although hand tools carry most of the burden in traditional furniture repair, there are several power tools that are highly useful, if not absolutely necessary: an electric or cordless drill, a bench grinder and a drill press (benchtop or floorstanding). Power saws with significant application in repair include the highly versatile band saw and the fast, powerful table saw. Most professional repair shops also are equipped with a lathe and a stationary sanding center, along with portable power sanders.

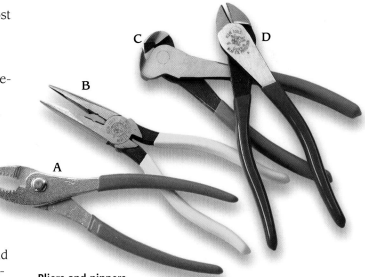

Pliers and nippers
are used mostly to remove metal fasteners. Above: (A) standard pliers, (B) needlenose pliers, (C) end nippers, and (D) side cutters.

Knives are versatile
tools you'll come to depend heavily upon in furniture repair work. The basic types you'll want include a pocket knife, a utility knife with replaceable blades, and a craft knife.

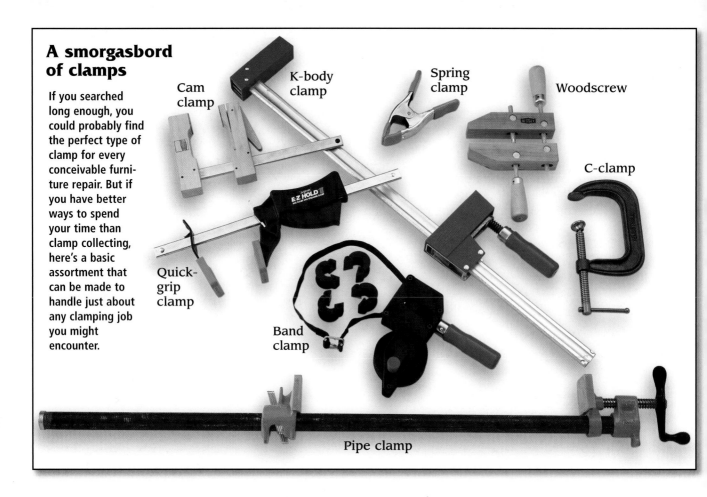

Cam clamp

K-body clamp

Spring clamp

Woodscrew

C-clamp

Quick-grip clamp

Band clamp

Pipe clamp

Clamps & clamping

Woodworkers have a saying: "You can never have enough clamps." Flip through any woodworking supply catalog and you'll find dozens of different types of clamps, from bar clamps to pipe clamps to C–clamps to strap clamps and on and on. There also are very specialized clamps available, but for the vast majority of furniture repair the clamps discussed here will get the job done.

C-clamps. A *C-clamp* has a cast-metal body in the shape of a *C.* The top of the *C* has a flat pad shape, while the other end has a threaded rod to which a sliding lever is attached. These are available in many different sizes, from just a couple of inches long up to 12 inches or so. C-clamps also come with a range of throat sizes (the maximum distance they can reach from the edge of a workpiece), from an inch or so on the small clamps up to 6 to 8 inches on *deep-throat clamps.* The metal pads on these clamps will leave indentations in wood, so they need to be covered with wooden or plastic protectors (See photo, next page).

Bar and pipe clamps. These essential clamps differ slightly in appearance but provide the same primary benefit: a long reach that makes them well suited for panel glue-ups. *Bar clamps* generally are sold as complete units with the clamp heads preattached to metal

bars of varying length. *Pipe clamps* are packaged with the clamp heads only: you supply the pipe (generally, black gas pipe is used). Bar/pipe clamps can differ slightly among manufacturers, but most are comprised of three parts, a stationary jaw with a crank or handle, a rigid bar or pipe, and a moveable jaw that rides on the bar or pipe. The handle is unscrewed all the way and the bar is placed across the width of the piece to be clamped. The sliding jaw is brought up to snug the clamp, then the screw is tightened at the other end to apply the clamping pressure. A variation of the typical bar clamp that's very effective is the *K-body clamp* with rectangular jaws that are encased in soft plastic. This allows the clamp to exert force over the entire jaw, eliminating the need for protective pads or wooden *cauls* to distribute clamping pressure more evenly. The down side of these clamps is their rather hefty price.

Woodscrews (sometimes called *twin-screw clamps*). This design incorporates two screws operating independently between two pieces of wood. When tightened, these clamps exert a great deal of pressure across the entire open width of the wooden jaws. While the large ones can become rather cumbersome to use, the smaller ones offer good control, making them a nice choice for more delicate tasks, such as attaching veneer patches.

CLAMPING TIPS

Use notched supports to lift pipe clamps off your worksurface. This provides clearance for adjusting the clamp heads and keeps the pipes from rolling around. Lay the workpiece to be clamped across the pipes.

Clamp pads are essential to prevent damaging the work-piece when you tighten the clamps. They're easiest to use when preattached to the clamp jaws (otherwise, you'll need an extra hand to hold clamp blocks in place as you tighten the clamps).

Band (strap) clamps. These clamps are really nothing more than a fabric belt that wraps completely around the object you want to clamp. One end has a ratcheting mechanism and a loop that you pass the other end of the strap through. The ratchet end is then tightened. This is a very effective way to clamp items like chairs and picture frames because the equalized pressure is applied to all the joints simultaneously. They can also clamp irregularly shaped items more effectively than most other clamp types.

Spring clamps. These inexpensive clamps are basically oversized clothespins, but they can exert plenty of force for gluing. They're quick and easy clamps for small jobs where you have to see precisely what you're doing—for example, when attaching drawer stops, or positioning thin or very delicate applied wood moldings.

Quick clamps (generically called *squeeze-ratchet clamps*). These handy clamps are first-rate for complicated glue-ups where you need a free hand to hold the parts together while you use the other hand to install and

tighten the clamp. These clamps can also be operated in reverse, which is helpful for getting joints apart.

Cam clamps. Cam clamps are excellent (but little-known) problem-solving clamps. They're built like a bar clamp, with one sliding and one stationary jaw, (typically wood) and the sliding wooden jaw has a cam lever that swings upward to tighten the clamp. The jaws are lined with cork, which allows these clamps to clamp round and other non-square surfaces. The primary advantage of these clamps is their deep throat capacity, which can reach over 7 in.

"Found" clamps. Some items found around the house are useful as clamps for complicated profiles and shapes. Electrical or duct tape, large rubber bands, shrink wrap and bicycle inner tubes can be put into service as strap clamps. To use an inner tube, poke a hole and start cutting with scissors at an angle of around 30°. Cut along the entire length and you'll eventually wind up with a long, 2-in.-wide strip of rubber. Tie one end and stretch the rubber around the object you want to clamp.

Tips for successful clamping

- It's important to go through a dry clamping run before you apply glue and start clamping. Make sure the pieces to be glued fit together as closely as possible. A general rule of thumb is that if you have to apply a lot of clamping pressure to close the joint, the glue probably won't hold it together very well. Run through the entire clamping operation, check everything for a good fit and then remove the clamps, placing them near the work area in the reverse order in which you'll use them.
- Have plenty of water on hand (alcohol if you're using epoxy) to wipe up drips. You'll also need clean rags and plenty of room to maneuver.
- Apply enough glue so that you get a little squeeze-out (little beads of glue are best). Glue will act as a lubricant and the parts may squirm out of position a bit, so you may need to use additional clamps to counteract the pull of the main clamps.
- When using clamps with no protective pads on the jaws or heads, use solid wood scraps as clamping pads. Have plenty of the scraps close at hand, and consider waxing them beforehand so they won't stick to the wood or the finish.

A **quality corded drill** has multiple uses, including drilling holes and, when fitted with special bits, grinding, smoothing and shaping. It can be used to drive screws as well, but is not as effective in this task as cordless drill/drivers.

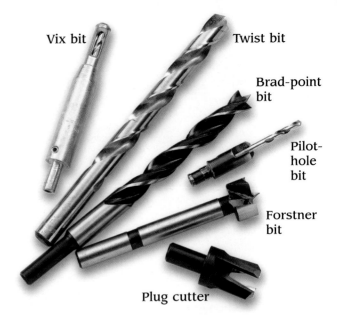

Vix bit   Twist bit

Brad-point bit

Pilot-hole bit

Forstner bit

Plug cutter

Drill bits & accessories expand the number of jobs a drill can manage. In addition to complete sets of quality drill bits (including twist bits, brad-point bits and Forstner bits) look for a Vix bit to help you center screws in hardware, a pilot-hole bit, counterboring bit (not shown) and a plug cutter. Also pick up a good set of drill/driver bits.

Power tools

The standard stationary and portable power tools can certainly be of help in furniture repair, including a table saw, band saw, jig saw, circular saw, router and power sanders. But for most repair work, drills and a bench grinder are the critical power tools you'll need.

Drills. If you could have only one drill in your shop, the best choice for most people would be a *corded electric drill.* It will produce more torque and power than most cordless drills and likely will be less expensive.

A benchtop drill press has comparable power and capacity to a floor-standing model, but with a smaller footprint and price tag.

Corded drills are made with different chuck sizes, including ¼-, ⅜- and ½-in. The most common is ¼-in., which is fine for most repair work you'll run into. If you don't have a drill, buy one with a ⅜-in. chuck, a reversing switch and variable speed. The other specification on drills is motor amperage. From 4 to 5 amps is about average for a good quality drill. When it comes to *cordless drills,* there is a dizzying array of choices. The beefy, high voltage cordless drills that compete in torque with the corded versions are rather heavy and awkward to use for

more delicate drilling. Look for a drill with a mid-range voltage battery (12 volts is a good choice) to handle general drilling and driving of screws.

Drill press. The drill press is used for drilling tasks that are either too awkward or too dangerous to attempt with a portable drill. In addition, a drill press will cut a perfectly straight hole. For drilling metal, nothing beats a drill press (set on low speed) fitted with a carbide-tipped twist bit. A benchtop drill press is perfectly fine for most drilling tasks and in repair work, and they occupy much less space than a floorstanding drill press.

Drill bits. Standard *twist bits* are good all-purpose bits for drilling holes in both wood and metal. *Brad-point bits* have a small spur point at the tip, which centers it more accurately than a twist bit and prevents it from wandering off your mark. *Forstner bits* will cut holes with smoother sides and a flat bottom, and also are very good for drilling into end grain. *Plug cutters* are the best tools for making wood plugs to fill counterbores and cover screw heads.

Bench grinder. For sharpening and grinding, nothing beats a bench grinder. Prices vary on these: pick one that suits your budget, but keep in mind that the grinding wheels do vary in both price and performance.

Tools You Can Make or Modify

There are some situations you'll run into that require either the use of specialized furniture repair tools or common tools that have been modified to accomplish a particular task. Unless you have a large budget for acquiring expensive tools you'll only use a couple of times, making your own is always a nice option to have. Some of the make-it-yourself tools shown here are fashioned mostly from scraps you'll find lying around the shop. Others are made by modifying tools. Such cases are one of the few times when it might be wise to disregard the golden rule of buying tools: Buy the best tool you can afford. Because you'll be rendering it useless for other tasks, go ahead and pick up the cheapest version of the tool you can find.

Screw extractor

Screw extractors (not to be confused with reverse-thread screw extractor bits) cut a hole around the head of a recessed nail or screw so it can be removed more easily (they can also be used to provide access to a screw or nail that has no head). Several sizes are usually needed. Since the commercial models tend to be expensive, try making your own from cutoff pieces of narrow-diameter tubing, as shown below.

A screw extractor can be fashioned from pieces of metal tubing to bore out the wood around stripped or broken fasteners. The teeth at the cutting end are cut with a metal file. Before using the extractor, insert a dowel into the noncutting end of the tubing to keep it from distorting when chucked into your drill.

HOW TO MAKE A SCREW EXTRACTOR

1 Choose a piece of tubing with an inside diameter that's slightly larger than the head of the fastener you're removing and cut off a 2-in. length. Fit a piece of wooden doweling inside the tubing (you may need to whittle a dowel that's a bit too thick down to size).

2 Holding the tube gently in a vise so you don't flatten it, use a hacksaw or triangular file to cut "teeth" into the open end.

HOW TO USE A SCREW EXTRACTOR

1 To use the extractor, you'll need a guide block to start and support it while cutting. Make this from a 1-in.-thick piece of hardwood by drilling a hole through block that's matched to the outside diameter of the extractor. Clamp the block to the workpiece with the guide hole aligned over the fastener head. Chuck the extractor into a drill and drill down past or near the tip of the fastener.

2 Withdraw the extractor bit. Often, the "plug" containing the screw will come out with the extractor. If not, grab it with needlenose pliers, snap it off and remove it.

Scratch stock

A scratch stock is a homemade cutting and profiling tool you can use to duplicate just about any beading or profiled edge. The scratch stock consists of a wooden handle (the stock), made from an L-shaped piece of hardwood then cut in two. Start with two identical pieces of hardwood scrap, approximately 2 × 5 in. Stack the workpieces on top of one another, with the edges aligned. Fasten them together with four 1¼-in. wood screws driven through pilot holes (See photo, above). Lay out a 1 × 3-in. notch on one end then cut out the notch. Smooth the inside cuts, as these will ride against the piece you're cutting. The stock holds a cutter fashioned from very hard steel—an old saw or scraper blade works well to make it. The blade is ground and filed to a reverse profile of the required molding.

Here are some pointers for making a scratch stock:

• Use larger or smaller wood scraps to make the stock, as needed. The wood blanks should be at least 4 to 6 inches longer than the molding you need.

• The blank will dull after a bit, but you can sharpen it with a few light touches from a small, fine file.

HOW TO MAKE A SCRATCH-STOCK CUTTER

1 Make the scratch stock that holds the profile cutter as described at left. To make a cutter, cut a piece of hard steel to about 1 × 2 in. (you can use an old saw blade if you like; we used a small piece of 1½-in.-wide strap iron). Apply dark paint to the steel so the white cutting lines will be more visible.

4 Refine the shape with a single-cut metal file, then sharpen the edges of the profile.

Make good use of small hardwood scraps by cutting them into wedge shapes you can use for breaking wood joints and making repairs.

Wedges

Wooden wedges are used primarily to dismantle joints that won't come apart easily. Make them in a variety of thicknesses and lengths from hardwood scraps (maple is a good choice). Cut the wedges so the grain runs lengthwise, not across the width (called short-grain). Round over the edges of the wedges, particularly the thin end, and coat them with shellac followed by paste wax to reduce friction. The

2 To get the reverse image of the molding, you'll need a cross-section of the original molding. If you have to cut off a small piece, go ahead. Set the piece of molding onto the steel blank and trace around the profile with a scratch awl.

3 Grind away the portion of the metal blank that was beneath the molding when you scribed the blank—this will create the reverse profile you need. Use a bench grinder.

6 To use the scratch stock and cutter, cut a workpiece from the same species of wood as the furniture part you're replacing. Secure the workpiece and drag the cutter over one edge repeatedly until the profile is cut. Trim the workpiece to width and thickness on your table saw, then cut it to length.

5 Insert the profiled and sharpened cutter between the two halves of the scratch stock—you'll need to loosen or remove the screws first. Tighten the screws to secure the cutter.

smaller wedges are used singly or in pairs to coax apart stubborn joints, while the larger ones can be used to remove tops attached with glue blocks. For best results, position wedges on opposite sides of a joint and drive each a little at a time before switching to the other. Use a wood or urethane mallet to drive the wedges—a metal hammerhead will destroy them.

Break apart stubborn glue joints by driving hardwood wedges into the joint from multiple directions.

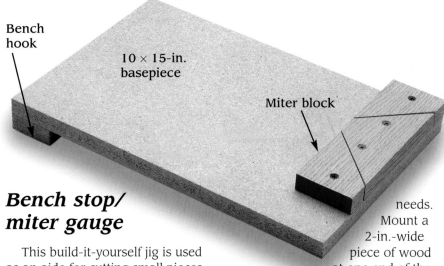

Bench hook

10 × 15-in. basepiece

Miter block

Bench stop/ miter gauge

This build-it-yourself jig is used as an aide for cutting small pieces of wood at right angles or 45° miters. Typically, it will have a 10 × 15-in. basepiece made of plywood or particleboard, but you can re-size the dimensions to suit your needs. Mount a 2-in.-wide piece of wood at one end of the basepiece. Turn the base over and mount a 2½-in.-wide hardwood block on the other end. Make the block 2 in. shorter than the width of the base, and make sure your end cut is perfectly straight and square, as this will be a guide for making 90° cuts. Once the block is fastened on both ends, measure in 1 in. at each end of the top edge, and draw two 45° lines inward. Cut through the block along the 45° lines, guiding the saw with a guide block, if necessary, to make accurate 45° cuts.

To use the bench stop/miter gauge, you simply hook the uncut block over the edge of a bench and hold or clamp the jig in place. Draw a cutting line on the work-piece then set it against the cutting block so the line aligns with the straight or 45° slot. Clamp the workpiece in place and make your cut with a back saw.

HOW TO MAKE A BENCH STOP/MITER GAUGE

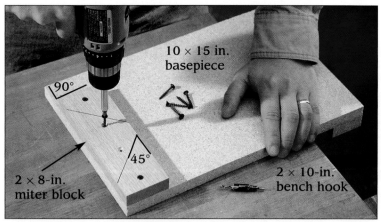

10 × 15 in. basepiece

90°

45°

2 × 8-in. miter block

2 × 10-in. bench hook

1 Attach a piece of hardwood (the miter block) about 2 × 8 in. to one end of a 10 × 15 plywood or particleboard basepiece. Draw 45° lines across the block as on a miter box. Attach a 2 × 10-in. wood block (the bench hook) to the opposite end of the basepiece on the opposite face.

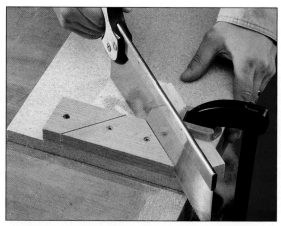

2 With the miter block mounted to the basepiece (all the edges should be square and aligned), cut through the block along each of the miter lines. Clamp a guide next to the line to ensure a straight cut.

Sanding boards & blocks

Make up a few sanding boards and blocks for your hand-sanding chores. With the sanding boards, a sheet of sandpaper is attached to the board with spray-on adhesive, then the workpiece is rubbed back and forth across the paper. The board should be large enough (around 24 × 24 in.) that it can be clamped to a worksurface. Make sanding blocks in a variety of sizes (the one to the left is about 3 × 14 in.).

Nail puller

This clever tool is made by modifying a pair of end nippers (buy an inexpensive pair—they'll get chewed up a bit, but you can easily regrind them). The first step is to grind the outside bevel off the face, using a bench grinder. Follow the natural curve of the nippers, if they have one, or put a slight curve on them if they don't. This may require a bit of work. Periodically cool the tool by dipping it in water, or you'll destroy the temper of the steel. Grind until there's no outside bevel left.

The nail puller is used to dig out nails or staples that are flush with or slightly above the wood surface. To use the tool, grab the fastener securely with the jaws and gently rock the tool to pull up the fastener. Pull it up a little, grab the fastener farther down the shank, then pull it up again. Squeeze the handles just enough to grab the fastener. Because there's an inside cutting bevel, you'll risk cutting the soft steel, so take it easy. When the edges of the jaws become nicked or damaged, you can file them flat with a small file, working from the inside. Eventually, you'll grind enough metal so that the tool no longer closes, at which time you'll need to make a new pair (which is why buying an inexpensive pair of nippers makes

An ordinary pair of end nippers (usually used for cutting wire and removing wire staples) can be converted to a highly effective nail puller simply by grinding away part of the jaws.

sense). You can generally find end nippers in the electrical tools section of your local hardware store.

MAKING & USING A NAIL PULLER

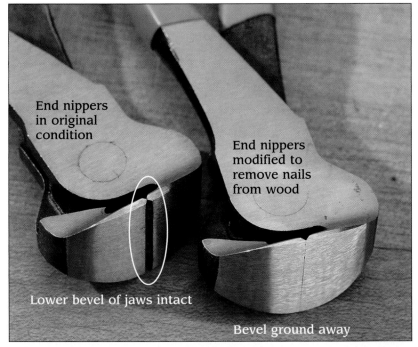

End nippers in original condition

End nippers modified to remove nails from wood

Lower bevel of jaws intact

Bevel ground away

This nail puller is made by grinding away the bottoms of the jaws on a pair of end nippers to remove the lower bevel where the nipper jaws meet (left photo). This allows you to rest the jaws so the "grabbing" portion of the jaws is flush on the wood surface. Once this is done, you can easily grab a small nailhead that's protruding just the slightest amount above the wood surface (right photo). Rock the tool back and forth to pull up the nail, regripping it farther down the shaft as it is extracted.

White and yellow glue are by far the most common types used in woodworking and furniture repair. Technically called "PVA glues" (which stands for polyvinyl acetate) they are also known as "carpenter's glue," "wood glue" or by their various brand names.

PVA Glues

PVA (polyvinyl acetate) glues are the most common woodworking glues and can be divided further into two types: *white* and *yellow* glue (generally called *carpenter's glue* or *wood glue*). They are an emulsion of polyvinyl acetate resin in water. They are inexpensive, non-toxic and easy to use. White glues, like *Elmer's School Glue,* are often dismissed as poor glues for wood, but they are just as strong as their yellow counterparts. And on the positive side, they have a slightly longer open time which makes them good for complex assemblies or for veneer work. On the negative side, they are rather runny and do not sand well because they soften easily under heat. Yellow PVA's were originally formulated to overcome the negative aspects of white glue. They are as close to an all-purpose woodworking glue as you can get. *Franklin's Titebond* and *Elmer's Carpenter's Wood Glue* are examples of this type. Yellow glues are essentially white glues that have been modified to have better woodworking properties. They are less runny because they are thicker and have a higher solids content (the ratio of resin to solvent). They sand better because the resin is harder and consequently doesn't gum up and clog sandpaper. Yellow glues do have several minor disadvantages you need to take into consideration, however. They have a short open time of around five minutes, so you have to work quickly with them. They also have a high initial tack, which makes repositioning parts and joints difficult.

Crosslinking PVA's. These are the newest PVA's on the market. They were formulated to overcome the biggest objection to ordinary PVA's—their poor moisture resistance. Crosslinking PVA glues can be used on outdoor furniture and projects that come into contact with a lot of water vapor. They handle very much like regular yellow PVA's, with the only differences being that they are thicker and a different color. *Titebond II* is a crosslinking PVA with a slightly darker amber color and higher viscosity and solids content than original *Titebond. Borden's* crosslinking product is a dark brown color and is gel-like in consistency, which keeps it from dripping.

Glues & gluing

For furniture repair work, you'll find hundreds of different brand names of glues that are suitable. At least half of these have been introduced in the past 25 years. Unfortunately, there is no single glue that is perfect for every repair situation. Consequently, confusion may arise when selecting the appropriate glue for the job at hand. Adding to this confusion is the notion that some glues are vastly superior to others. This is simply not true. Most glues will form an adequate bond that is stronger than the wood itself. But each type of glue has working characteristics that do make it better than others for certain applications.

There are five general categories of glues suitable for woodworking (and, by extension, furniture repair).

They are *PVA glues* (polyvinyl acetate), *epoxy, liquid hide glue, granular hide glue* and *super glue* (cyanoacrylate). Each of these types is featured within this chapter. There are other glues that eventually crop up in discussion of woodworking glues, but they do not bond well enough to be useful in general wood furniture repair. These include *hot-melt glues,* which will temporarily attach pieces together for jigs and fixtures, and *contact cement.* Contact cement is sometimes recommended for veneering, but PVA or hide glue is better for this purpose.

Before getting too deeply into the strengths, weaknesses and differences between glue types, it helps to have a better understanding of how glue works.

How glue works. Two forces are at work in any glue joint. One is *adhesion*—the molecular force that makes the glue stick to the wood. For many years, it was assumed that the adhesive formed tiny hardened tendrils within the porous structure of the wood that locked the two pieces of wood together. This *mechanical adhesion* does play a small role in forming the glue joint, but current scientific opinion is that a different type of force called *specific adhesion* is much more important. Specific adhesion results from strong molecular attraction between the wood and the glue. For this to occur, the adhesive must penetrate the wood cells and "wet" the fibers. The second force acting on a glue joint is *cohesion*—the force that makes the glue stick to itself. This is the solid glue "line" in a joint. Cohesion is strongest when the two pieces to be joined are machined so they mate as closely as possible. This results in a glue line that may only be a few thousandths of an inch thick.

Understanding adhesion and cohesion is important when dealing with glues and repair work because it explains the two requirements for good gluing. The first requirement, thorough "wetting" of the wood fibers with the glue (to promote specific adhesion), demands that the wood be very clean. Glue can't penetrate through wax, dirt or old glue (except for animal hide glue). The second requirement is that the two pieces of wood fit together as closely as possible (to promote cohesion). Glues, with the exception of epoxy, cannot fill a gap in a poor-fitting joint and still provide strength, so sometimes joints will need to be re-cut or trimmed to get a good glue bond. In the case of old furniture, many joints fail simply because the wood shrinks and the glue cannot provide the strength necessary to hold the wood together.

Glue applicators

Applicators make gluing a lot easier, cleaner and faster. They can also allow you to get glue into crevices and spaces you couldn't otherwise reach. Here are some useful glue applicators:

Syringes. These are invaluable for getting glue into tight areas or injecting under pressure. They can also be used to get solvents into joints for deactivating glues. There are two types: medical-type syringes for injecting low viscosity glues like white glue and thinned hide glue, as well as solvents like water, vinegar and alcohol; and high-pressure syringes that inject glues with great force. The high-pressure syringes have grips you curl your first two fingers around while your thumb is used to push down on a plunger. The tip is usually brass, which unscrews, and the plunger comes out to make cleaning easy. The rubber o-ring may eventually deteriorate, but can be replaced.

Palette knives. Artist's palette knives are used for mixing two-part glues that require blending, such as epoxy. They're also first-rate for getting glues under blistered veneer or other areas that are hard to reach with a brush. In a pinch, wooden stirring sticks or tongue depressors can be used instead.

Glue brushes. Metal-shafted glue brushes are good general-purpose glue applicators. They're sold primarily for applying flux before soldering, but most woodworking stores sell them for use with glue. They're too big for precise application in small areas, but you can purchase cheap artist's brushes for this purpose. Glues will usually ruin these brushes quickly. Large, inexpensive paintbrushes can be used for application of glues over large areas, as can trim paint rollers.

Glue bottles. The bottle that the glue is sold in makes a pretty good applicator, assuming you're not buying it by the gallon. For applying glue to edges of boards, nothing beats a *glue roller applicator,* which is a hard rubber or plastic roller that mounts onto a plastic glue bottle. When turned over, the bottle dispenses glue to the roller.

Roller applicator

Original bottle

Artist's palette knife

Syringes

Glue brush

Tips for working with glue. There is an old saying in woodworking that glues don't fail, only woodworkers do. This is absolutely true. A well-executed glue joint will probably never fail under normal use. But unfortunately, much can go wrong during the gluing process that will contribute to joint failure.

The pointers below will ensure better gluing success.

• The number one cause of glue joint failure is ill-fitting joints. Remember that the glue has to penetrate or "wet" the fibers of the wood to achieve specific adhesion. Try to achieve as close a fit as possible. This may require rebuilding

Super glue is used for minor patching jobs, like reattaching small pieces of veneer, that require strong, quick adhesion. But the brittle bond super glues make are not suitable for structural joints.

Super glue

Cyano-acrylate glues, commonly called *superglues*, are a relatively new glue for woodworkers. They cure instantly, form waterproof bonds and do not need clamping. They are invaluable for repairs to small pieces of inlay and veneer, and the thinned varieties of these glues will actually wick into small cracks through capillary action. But on the downside, they are expensive and they cure to an extremely brittle bond. This is bad in situations where joints are placed under stress, such as chair rungs and mortise-and-tenon joints. The joint will break apart easily with a sharp rap or knock.

Manufacturers sell cyano-acrylates in several viscosity levels, each designed for different gluing situations. They also sell an *activator* or *chemical accelerator* that can be sprayed on one of the parts to speed up the curing process.

Getting a Grip on Glue Terminology

Here are some terms used to describe physical features of glues, along with a few things you should know about each term.

Shelf Life. The period of time that a glue remains usable after manufacture. Shelf life can be hard to determine, but as a rule, if the normal working properties of the glue as stated on the package are different from what you're experiencing, the glue is probably past its shelf life. The yellow and white glues, called *PVAs* (polyvinyl acetate), and pre-mixed *liquid hide glue* have shelf lives of up to 12 months if stored in airtight containers. Glues that require mixing (*epoxies, plastic resin*) have a long shelf life in unmixed form. *Cyano-acrylate glue* (super glue) has a shelf life of about a year, in most cases. Dry *hide glue flakes* have an indefinite shelf life.

Pot life. This is the amount of time a glue remains usable after mixing. Two-part glues, such as *plastic resin* and *epoxy,* have pot lives that vary from five to 30 minutes. Colder temperatures extend pot life.

Open assembly time. The period of time you have between spreading the glue on the surface and the point at which it starts to set. *White glues* have a slightly longer open assembly time than *yellow glues.* *Hide glue* made from solids dissolved in water and then heated will gel quickly, while pre-mixed *liquid hide glue* has a fairly long open time. This feature is important because some assemblies that need to be glued up all at once require a glue with a long open assembly time to allow enough time for assembly and clamping.

Closed assembly time. The amount of time needed under clamping for the glue to set. This is a big source of confusion among woodworkers. Most woodworkers think that clamps need to be left on until the glue cures (usually overnight). But in general, clamps can be removed after the glue has set enough so removing the clamps will not disturb the joint. This is about three times the maximum open assembly time, but most manufacturers recommend slightly longer clamp times. *PVA glues* usually require only an hour under clamping.

Glue set. The condition at which the glue is gelled enough to be capable of holding the pieces together after the clamps are removed. The glue is not completely dry at this point and pieces should be set aside undisturbed until the final cure.

Glue cure. The amount of time it takes for the glue to completely cure to form maximum bond strength. As an example, *Titebond* will set enough within one hour to remove clamps, but will take at least 24 hours to completely cure. Some *epoxies* and *urea-formaldehyde glues* can take up to four days to cure.

the joint, as will be explained later.

• Dry-clamp joints before gluing. This helps you avoid surprises during the actual glue-up. It also lets you know exactly which clamps and cauls you'll need so you don't have to take time searching for them during the actual glue-up.

• After cutting the joints, keep the wood clean. Oils from your hands, wax and oils on the glue-up bench all can get onto freshly cut surfaces and contaminate the joint.

• Apply the right amount of glue. You should only have small beads of glue squeeze out during clamping. Too much glue is wasteful, and too little can cause starved joints. Using small brushes to precisely apply glue to small areas helps you avoid messy joints.

• Pay attention to grain direction. The strongest joints are formed by gluing edge to edge or long grain to long grain. Gluing end grain to end grain is impossible. End grain to long grain should also be avoided.

• Watch your pressure. When clamping, apply just enough pressure to close the joint and stop when

Polyurethane glue

Polyurethane glues are used to bond a variety of materials, including wood, metal and ceramics. Because poly glue expands when it sets, it can cause problems when used to repair wood joints. The squeeze-out forms a foam that's difficult to remove from almost everything it touches, including skin. Wear disposable gloves, and wipe up spills immediately with a rag and mineral spirits or acetone. **Warning: Polyurethane glue should only be used with excellent ventilation. Asthmatics and people with chronic lung conditions should not use this product.**

Epoxy

Epoxy is the best choice for gluing poorly fitting joints or joints that will undergo prolonged immersion or contact with water. They are solvent resistant, do not shrink, have excellent gap-filling ability and high solids means parts can be assembled without using clamps. They are generally available in *5-minute* and *slow-set* versions, but the final cure can take anywhere from 24 hours up to a week. Uncured and gelled epoxies can be cleaned up with alcohol, but no chemical will dissolve cured epoxy (don't use it on wooden pieces that may need to be dismantled at a later date).

The major advantage of epoxies is that they do not lose bonding power when they are used for gap filling. Other glues fail in this regard. Another application for epoxies is gluing oily woods, like teak, rosewood and cocobolo.

For repair work, epoxy is a good choice because the clear resin and hardener can be mixed with anything from sawdust to powdered pigments to blend the dried glue with the surrounding surface. You can also adjust the mixing ratio to achieve different cured resin properties. More resin will increase the hardness and tensile strength, while more hardener

will increase the elasticity of the cured glue. Many manufacturers sell additives for epoxies. You can purchase anti-sag additives to keep the epoxy from running before it is cured. There are also fillers which will make the epoxy act like putty.

When using epoxy, apply just enough pressure to bring the parts together. The minimum thickness for a strong epoxy joint is 0.005 in., about double that required for other glues. And be aware that epoxy is toxic during mixing and application, so wear gloves when using it. The cured bond is non-toxic.

Epoxy stick (left) is cut into chunks and kneaded to combine parts then used as a wood filler. **Two-part epoxy syringe** (middle) ensures that equal parts of hardener and resin are delivered to mixing vessel for blending. **Two-part epoxy containers** (right) are the most economical format for purchasing the glue.

Hide glue is an ancient bonding agent that is seldom used today, except by restorationists. But both the dry granular and ready-to-use versions have several useful properties that make them worth considering.

Hide glue

Hide glue was the principal adhesive used to make furniture up until the late 1940s. It's produced by immersing the hides of animals (usually cattle) in hot water to extract *collagen*, which is processed further to yield glue. Hide glue product is available in pre-mixed, ready-to-use form or in dry granular form. The granules are activated into glue by mixing them with water under heat.

Hide glue is the only glue that possesses the unique property of readhering to itself: it will melt the old hide glue and form a new permanent bond. The downside of hide glue is that it is not particularly moisture- and heat-resistant. This general disadvantage can be viewed as an advantage in some situations, however. Conservators and restorers of valuable antiques use hide glue because these pieces may be taken apart at a later date. Also, in some cases where veneer has blistered or bubbled and was glued with hide glue, it's sometimes possible to simply apply heat and moisture to restick the veneer in place.

Hide glue made from dry granules has another downside in that it has a very short open assembly time, especially in cold, dry weather. The open assembly time can be extended by adding table salt or urea to the hot glue (add about a tablespoon of either substance to each cup of prepared glue).

Pre-mixed, ready-to-use hide glue contains gel suppressant and preservative chemicals to extend the open time and protect the glue from bacterial decay. These chemicals also create a long open assembly time, which is important if you need plenty of time to position all the pieces for regluing. While some restorers have suggested that the pre-mixed hide glues are not as strong as granular hide glue, it is generally agreed that both products have more than adequate bonding strength for furniture repair.

One word of caution: both types of hide glue will crystallize on contact with alcohol, which is an ingredient in many furniture strippers and is used to neutralize some others. Old furniture that has been stripped may need regluing.

HOW TO MIX HIDE GLUE FROM GRANULES

Dissolve the dry granules in the appropriate amount of water (left photo), as instructed by the manufacturer. After soaking for about 30 minutes the glue will absorb the water and swell to a jelly-like mass that is heated, typically in glue pots (look for glue pots in woodworking stores and catalogs). The pot will heat the mixture to around 140°F. Stir the mixture as it heats up. When ready to use, the hide glue should be about the thickness of honey (right photo). You may need to add water periodically to maintain the proper thickness.

beads of glue squeeze out. Aim for uniform clamping pressure. If you have to bear down very tightly on one specific clamp, it's a sure sign that the joint doesn't mate well.

Determining old glue type. Knowing what type of glue originally was used is very important when repairing furniture. The main reason is that hide glue, in particular, will rebond to itself but no other kind of glue will. When re-gluing, if any glue other than hide glue was used, you'll need to clean off all the old glue so the new glue can penetrate the wood. Hide glue was the most prevalent glue used in furnituremaking up until the late 1940s. So if you know the age of the furniture or can date it, you can often make a good educated guess as to what kind of glue was used.

You can identify hide glue by its characteristic color if you can find some glue squeeze-out. It's tan and as it ages it gets darker and very brittle. You can also test to see what glue was used. Brush some hot water on the old glue and wait several minutes. If the glue gets sticky, then it's hide glue. If it turns white or milky looking, it's a PVA glue. Chances are, it's one or the other. If it doesn't turn white or get sticky it's most likely epoxy or some other type of modern glue.

HOW TO DISSOLVE A GLUE JOINT

Very often in furniture repair you'll need to disassemble a joint or even an entire piece of furniture to make an effective and longlasting repair. Sometimes furniture joints come apart easily by hand or with gentle "persuasion" from a soft mallet. Other times, the joint can put up quite a fight. Rather than use greater force to break the joint (which can cause bigger problems than the one you're trying to fix), see if you can dissolve the glue holding the joint or joints together. The first step in doing this is to determine the type of glue you're dealing with (See above). Once you know which glue you have, you should be able to deactivate it with solvent.

Hide glue will soften by contact with hot water and will crystallize when contacted by alcohol. Hot water is usually safer, as alcohol will soften and strip a shellac finish. *PVA glues* will soften when exposed to hot vinegar. In either case, you'll have to get the solvent into the joint so it wets the glue. One way to accomplish this is simply by wiggling a joint that's already somewhat loose. If the joint is tight, you'll need to drill a small entrance hole or series of holes to get solvent inside. These should be drilled on the least visible side of the joint, using a 3/32-in. drill bit. You can then inject solvent with a glue syringe (the high-pressure syringes work best).

Once the solvent has been introduced into the joint, let it work for several minutes, then try wiggling the joint. Keep at it until the joint loosens enough that you can work more solvent in on all sides. Then disassemble the joint by hand or with a soft mallet.

HOW TO DISSOLVE GLUE IN A TIGHT JOINT

1 To create a path for the solvent (hot water or vinegar) to contact the glue, drill several 3/32-in. holes into the joint in a low-visibility area.

2 Inject the solvent into the entry holes with a high-pressure glue syringe. Repeat as needed until the joint loosens enough that you can inject additional solvent on all sides. Wiggle the mating parts gently until the joint is loose.

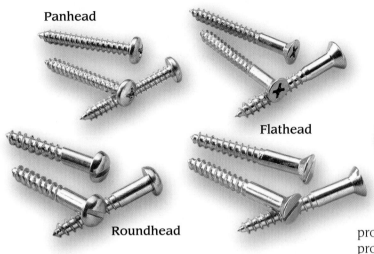

Panhead

Flathead

Roundhead

Square drive

Wood screws are classified by, among other things, the type and shape of the driver bit used to screw them in, and the general shape of the screw head. Panhead, roundhead and flathead screws are shown here. Slotted-head and phillips-head are the most common drive types, but you may run into square-drive screws on newer furnishings.

Fasteners

The purpose of fasteners in furnituremaking is to provide a mechanical connection that can accomplish several things: it can reinforce a glue joint and keep parts securely in place while the glue sets; or it may function as the sole connection when glue is not used, generally due to concern over wood movement, as when attaching a tabletop. Screws and nails are also used to attach corner blocks in chairs, which reinforces the joints. Good furniture employs a combination of sound joinery using glue in addition to fasteners.

Unfortunately, fasteners are often employed as a quick fix where proper regluing would have been a better solution. Loose joints are sometimes "stabilized" with metal brackets, which results in unsightly screw holes left behind after proper repairs are done. Split wood is frequently nailed or screwed and glued instead of being reglued using the proper clamps.

Screws. Screws are classified according to the type of slot, the shape of the head, the diameter and the length.

Slotted screws: Flathead screws are the oldest type of screws and have a straight slot in the head. These screws started showing up in the late 1700s and were made entirely by hand. Mass-production machines were invented in the mid 1850s and the flathead screw has been pretty much unchanged up to the present day.

Specialty screws you may encounter in furniture repair include hanger bolts (above) and lag screws (below).

Phillips-head screws. Phillips screws are found on furniture produced in the 1950s and later. They provide a more positive drive and are better suited to production woodworking. They'll grip better in a driver so you don't need to support them with your free hand.

Square-drive screws are a more recent screw-type innovation than phillips screws, even though they were invented in the early 1900s in Canada. They require a square-drive bit, and will drive you nuts if you don't have one. They are the modern screw design of choice. A hybrid design that's a combination of phillips and square drive (called *torx*) may also be encountered.

In addition to driving method, screws vary in the shape of the head. They may be *flathead, pan-shaped, domed* or *tapered.* Pan-shaped and dome-shaped lay above the wood, while tapered, bugle-head screws are countersunk below or flush to the surface. Flathead can be either flush or countersunk. The diameter of the screw is indicated by the *gauge* numbering system, with most woods screws falling between 6 and 12 gauge (designated by a # sign). The length is expressed in inches, from the tip to the top of the head. Common lengths are between ¾ and 3½ in.

Screws need a pilot hole so they wont split the wood when they're installed, especially near an end. A general rule is to use a drill bit that's roughly the same diameter as the *shank* (the solid shaft of metal that's between the threads of the screw). In addition, use the proper size driver to install the screw—the bit should fit snugly in the slot and not slip when you turn it. For older flathead screws, keep an old screwdriver you can regrind to the shape of the slot.

When using screws to join two pieces of wood together tightly, drive a pilot hole in the bottom piece and an oversized hole in the top piece. When the screw is tightened it acts like a clamp and will squeeze the two pieces together.

Specialty screws. There are at least two types of specialty screws you may run into. One is called a *hanger bolt* and has wood screw threads on one end and machine screw threads to accept a nut on the other. The typical place you find these is on table and chair legs. The wood screw part is driven into the wood leg, and the machine screw part goes through a hole in a bracket that's attached to a metal or wooden brace. If you ever need to install these, jam two nuts together by tightening them into each other, then drive the hangar bolt into the wood with the top nut. The other specialty screw is a *lag screw*. It's basically a hexhead screw with large screw threads. Like other screws, you need to drill a pilot hole the diameter of the shank to install them.

Nails are used to attach wood pieces together and can be used with or without glue. They're sometimes used as single point connectors for cross-grain attachment of solid wood backs to cabinets that would otherwise split if glued. They are available with or without heads. Headless nails are referred to as *finish nails* and are usually countersunk below the wood surface with a nailset. The length of nails is referred to by the small "d" or *penny* designation. Nails usually start at 2d and get longer as the pennyweight increases.

Brads are used to attach moldings and other small pieces of wood. Wire brads can be purchased with heads similar to nails or as headless brads which can be countersunk. In hardwoods, drill a pilot hole when attaching small, delicate moldings. Rather than searching for the exact size drill bit, simply snip off the head of the brad, chuck it in a drill and use it as the pilot "drill bit."

Dowels are short wood cylinders that are used to join wood parts together. They are simply small mortise-and-tenons in their concept. They revolutionized furnituremaking because they allowed for easier manufacturing of wooden parts. Pieces no longer needed to be cut oversized to accommodate the tenons on the ends, making both layout and design (as well as fabrication) much easier.

The first dowels were like our modern dowel rod, but this proved problematic. First of all, if the dowel

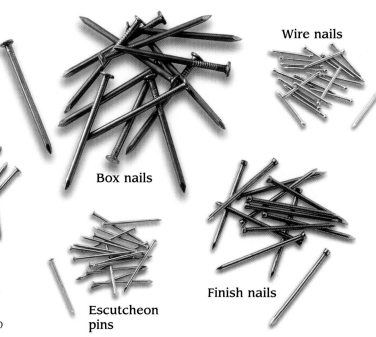

Box nails

Wire nails

Brads

Escutcheon pins

Finish nails

General types of nails and brads you'll use in furniture repair include brads, box nails, wire nails, finish nails and escutcheon pins for attaching hardware.

shrank at all, it lost good wood-to-wood contact. And second, when it was driven in, it forced the glue to the bottom and the dowel "bottomed out" without ever reaching wood. Modern dowels are grooved and compressed to allow an escape for glue squeeze-out, and they actually swell a bit, forming a tight lock on the wood.

You can purchase ready-made joinery dowels or use dowel rod. Dowel rod can be confusing because most of what's available is slightly undersized. Plus, you'll have to cut grooves in the cutoff pieces of dowel. If you absolutely have to use dowel rod, buy hardwood doweling.

Wood. The best way to repair wood is with more wood. So you'll need a stash of various pieces to use as parts or small repair pieces for furniture. This usually isn't a problem for most woodworkers, as they'll hang onto pieces of wood forever, but you may need to find pieces that match in grain and figure better than anything from the stock you have lying around.

If you need a piece of solid wood, you may try your local lumber mill or custom cabinet shop. Most of these places have piles or bins of "shorts" that are too small to be sold, and they'll happily part with them for a small price. Some places may even give them to you: they'll get rid of useless inventory and you'll usually find what you need.

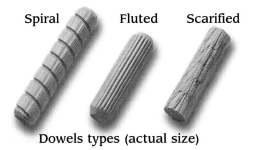

Spiral   Fluted   Scarified

Dowels types (actual size)

Dowels caused a revolution when they were first used for wood joinery, and they continue to be popular fasteners today. Spiral and fluted dowels designed specifically for joinery are preferable to ordinary dowel rod. If you do use dowel rod, scarify the surface with the jaws of a pliers to create a better glue bond in the dowel hole.

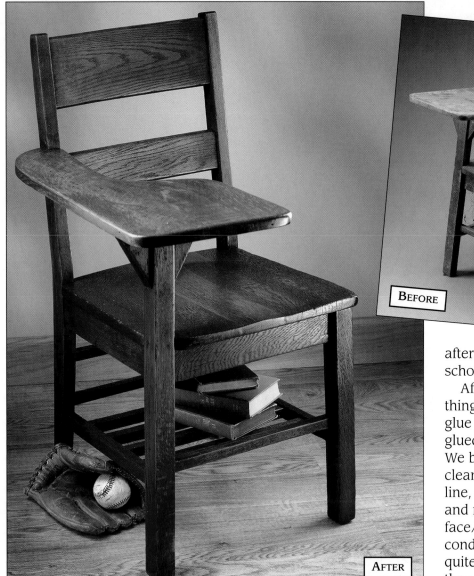

BEFORE

AFTER

Upgrading a School Desk

A little glue and a fresh finish were all the assistance this oak school desk needed to graduate from the detention hall to the honor roll.

You don't see desks made like this one anymore: at least not made with oak and strong wood joinery. And even with a broken glue-line in the seat board and a failed finish, restoring it looked to be as easy as A-B-C.

Regardless of age and type of joinery, most all-wood chairs should be disassembled and reglued as part of the restoration process. One or two sloppy joints create stress on the others, and repairing the bad joints can be done more effectively

after disassembly. And this school desk was no exception.

After we took the whole thing apart, we cleaned up the glue joints, then clamped and glued the frame back together. We broke the seat board cleanly along the failed glue line, scraped off the old glue, and reglued it. The writing surface/armrest was in decent condition, but had taken on quite a number of stains over the years.

We were able to clear up much of the staining with oxalic acid and sanding, although some of the discoloration had penetrated too deeply into the wood to be remedied without planing ¼ in. of wood off the top. But that was fine, since it was never our intention to try and make the desk look brand new. A dark walnut finish helped preserve the sense of age, and de-emphasized the blemishes slightly.

~MJ

(LEFT) *To start with, we completely dismantled the school desk so we could get at the mating parts of the joints, clean them up, and reglue and clamp them properly. With so many parts, it's very important to clearly label each part before you disassemble the project. We also broke apart the failed glue-line on the seat so we could clean up that joint, too. Then we reglued and clamped the seat.*

(RIGHT) Black stains on the armrest were most likely the result of water damage, although we preferred to think it was spilled ink. Bleaching the entire surface with an oxalic acid solution lightened the stains quite a bit, and sanding helped as well. Still, we weren't able to eliminate every trace, nor did we really want to.

(BELOW) We sanded all the parts— the grain on the armrest had raised from the bleaching solution, so it took a little extra sanding. Then we filled a few little nicks and dings with putty, sanded one more time, and applied a dark, rich wood stain and a tung oil topcoat.

Skills used in this project:

• *Regluing round mortise-and-tenon joints (pages 52 to 53)*

• *Glues & gluing (pages 24 to 29)*

• *Removing black stains (pages 124 to 125)*

• *Sanding (pages 118 to 121)*

• *Applying a finish (pages 128 to 155)*

Regluing is the solution to most furniture repair problems, yet it is seldom done using the proper techniques to ensure a long-lasting repair. Whether the problem is a loose joint, peeled veneer or cracks and splits in the wood, careful preparation, gluing and clamping will yield results that are as strong or stronger than before the damage or wear occurred. In the photo above, a picture frame with loose miter joints has been disassembled, cleaned and reglued. A web clamp (sometimes called a strap clamp) is used to hold the joints together until the glue sets.

Regluing

Most furniture repairs involve regluing. As we have discussed, joints in furniture fail for a variety of reasons inherent to the nature of wood, or due to general wear and tear, accidents or negligence. The first repair you'll likely ever run into may be something as simple as a loose rung on a chair, or as seemingly complex as a large veneer blister in the middle of your old dining table. Whatever the gluing operation may be, there are two basic principles to follow:

• **You must have clean wood so the new glue can penetrate.**
• **You must have good wood-to-wood contact for the joint to hold up.**

Regluing is a skill that's not just applied to furniture joints. You may also run into situations where you need to reglue cracks, splits or detached veneer. All of these repairs are covered in thorough detail in this chapter.

Performing durable repairs with glue also requires a good understanding of different glue products, application methods and clamping tools and strategies. Be sure to read the sections covering these subjects before attempting any regluing.

See pages **12 to 29** for more information on glues, gluing, clamping and dissolving glue joints.

Regluing wood joints

Along with accidental breakage, a glued furniture joint may loosen due to a variety of causes. The most common is simple everyday wear and tear, which produces racking stresses on the joint (like the back legs of a chair). Expansion and shrinkage due to changes in temperature or humidity are also leading causes of joint failure. These two forces may operate independently or together to produce failure at the glue line. A joint may also have been improperly or poorly cut when originally constructed, ultimately leading to failure of the joint. In most cases, you'll need to dismantle the affected joint (and often nearby ones) to make furniture repairs. "Quick-fix" repairs, like dribbling or injecting glues into joints, adding mending plates or nailing a loose joint seldom work. Instead, they usually result in the creation of new problems down the road.

To properly repair a furniture joint that's loose, you need to diagnose the extent of the problem. The easiest way to do this is to gently rack or twist the piece and see where the joinery is loose. For chairs, stand directly over the chair and grab the seat on each side. Twist the seat back and forth slightly. There will naturally be some give due to flexing of the wood. Pay attention to the undercarriage of the chair as you rack it. If you see stretchers pop in and out of mortises, it's a good sign that the base of the chair needs to be reglued. Also rack the back of the chair by twisting it slightly and wiggling the arms (if the chair has arms). As you do this, the wood should flex, but you should not be able to move components much. You can apply the same strategy to tables, desks and cabinets. Rack or twist the item, looking for unstained wood at the joints. Unstained wood is a sure sign that the joint has broken and regluing is in order. Excessive racking of cabinets and other furnishings with back panels can often be corrected simpy by reattaching or renailing the back panel.

Although glue does the bulk of the work in providing strength to a joint, most joints also utilize additional fastening devices. Many production-style, commercially manufactured furniture pieces are pinned with small finishing nails that were used to hold the glued joint together until the glue dried, eliminating the need for clamps. Glue blocks are often employed to counteract

Testing glue joints

Assess the condition of the glued joints in chairs and other furnishings by leaning lightly onto the furnishing and gently racking it back and forth and side to side. Expect some minor movement. If you can see joints actually separating you can be sure that regluing is required. Any signs of unstained wood at the joints also indicate a failed joint that needs regluing.

racking on chairs and to reinforce joinery on cabinets and casework. Whatever fasteners you encounter, they need to be removed during disassembly so the joint comes apart easily.

Removing nails. To pry out nails, you can use the screw extractor or reground end nippers (See pages 19 and 23) to get at nailheads set flush with the surface. If the nailheads are set below the surface, you have limited options for extracting them. You can dig around them with a small chisel or gouge, deep enough so you can get at the nailheads with a nail puller. Or, you can just leave them in place. This will cause the wood on the mating joint to split when the joint is pulled apart, but because it is hidden inside the joint, the split wood will be easier to repair "invisibly" than deep gouges that were dug in the exposed wood surface to get

Nail pullers are a great help in removing small nails. The pair shown here is made by regrinding a pair of electricians' end nippers. See page 23.

access to the nail-head.

Removing screws. When removing old flathead screws, make sure the tip of the screwdriver blade fits snugly into the screw slot (you may want to keep an old screwdriver around to regrind to size as needed—See page 12). If a screw is "frozen" in the joint, one way you may be able to loosen it is to position the tip of the screwdriver blade in the screw slot then heat the shank of the screwdriver with a propane torch (use an old screwdriver, preferably with a wood handle, and be sure to wear gloves). After the screw cools it should come out easily.

If you strip or break off a screw, use a *screw extractor* (See page 19) to bore around the screw head and down around the shank. Remove the broken screw

Heat up "frozen" screws

Removing screws that are stuck or "frozen" into a wood joint can be very aggravating, usually leading to a stripped screw head and a big mess. One trick that can "unstick" problem screws is to heat them with a propane torch. The heating and cooling will cause the screw to expand and contract, breaking the bond that's holding it in place. Insert an old screwdriver blade into the screw slot and carefully heat the shank of the tool to pass the heat onto the screw head.

and plug the hole with a dowel with the same grain direction as the wood.

If the joint was loose to begin with and you've removed all the fasteners, the joint should pull apart easily by hand. If not, there's probably a hidden fastener inside the joint. Look the joint over carefully for any telltale holes. If you can, slip a metal feeler gauge into the joint. In some instances, screws are counterbored and the hole plugged with wood from the same species. These can be hard to spot under a finish. If you encounter a screw plug, drill through the center of the plug with a small-diameter drill bit until you hit the head of the

HOW TO REMOVE A COUNTERBORED AND PLUGGED SCREW

1 If you encounter a screw that has been counterbored so the head is covered by a glued wood plug, the first step to remove the screw is to drill through the center of the plug until you hit the screw head.

2 Use a small wood chisel or gouge to pare away any remaining wood that's obstructing access to the screw head. Once you have a clear path to the screw it can be removed. After the repair is done, insert a new plug or fill the counterbore hole with wood putty.

screw. With a small, sharp gouge, neatly pare away the plug—avoid prying plugs out, as this will damage the shape of the hole and/or the wood surrounding it. Once you have access to the screw head, remove the screw. After repairing the joint replug the counterbore hole or fill it with wood putty (See page 122).

Dealing with stubborn joints. In some situations, a joint that is still properly or partially glued may need to be dismantled. If the mating parts of the joint can be wiggled, lightly tapping with a mallet and a piece of soft wood is usually enough to force the joint apart. If this doesn't work, inject some solvent into the joint (See page 29) and try again. In some cases, it may be necessary to deploy a bit more force to get a stubborn joint apart (but only do so as a last resort, when gentler methods have failed). Clamp manufacturers produce a reverse bar clamp, called a *spreader clamp,* that can be used to apply even force in an outward direction to force the mated part apart. Otherwise, an effective, economical and safe way to break a joint is with wood wedges (See pages 20 to 21). Size the wedges to the joint, and bear in mind that it's a good idea to use two wedges operating from different directions to equalize the pressure.

If you have a cabinetmaker's-style bench, you can place the workpiece between the bench dogs and run the tail of the vise in reverse. This will pull apart even the most stubborn joints on chairs. Remember to be patient with stubborn joints. With enough persistent wiggling and solvent to soften the glue, even the most tenacious joint comes apart. And the lesson from all that work is: understanding why good wood-to-wood contact makes for a very strong joint.

Once the joints are all apart, you can begin dismantling the furniture piece. Though it may seem easy to remember the sequence in which the parts go back together, it's always a good idea to label all the parts with the proper removal order and orientation notations. Just stick a piece of masking tape on each part and write on the tape. You can use a numbering sequence that's keyed to a diagram that you draw, or simply label the parts by name and place-ment (for example, *top stretcher, right*). NOTE: It's very important to mark "up" on chair rungs, as many of these are symmetri-cal, making them easy to reverse. Label all the parts before disassembly.

OPTIONS FOR BREAKING JOINTS

Spreader clamps apply outward force as you tighten the head. They are particularly helpful for restoration and refinishing work, where parts must be disassembled by breaking glue joints. Spreaders apply gradual, rather than high impact, force, which is far less damaging to parts and finishes.

Wood wedges cut from hardwood scraps can be driven into the joint from each side to break the bond. See page 21 for more information on making and using wedges.

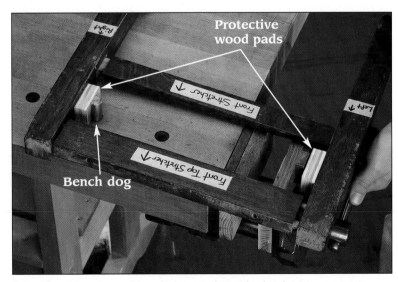

A **woodworking vise and bench dogs** can be used to break joints on some types of furniture assemblies.

Disassembling chairs: For a number of reasons, the furniture type that most often needs disassembly and regluing is the chair. Once you've labeled all the parts (See previous page), begin dismantling the chair. Most chairs follow one of two general designs. They are either a stool with a top arm and back support built on top (like a Windsor chair), or they are comprised of two full-height rear legs that form the back, which are attached to smaller front legs with stretchers and a seat. If your chair is a "stool" type, take the arms or top assembly off first, then take apart the base. If it's the full-height rear leg type, remove the seat (if you can), and remove the glue blocks. These are usually held on with glue and screws. The blocks may be popped off by striking down on the glue joint with a paint scraper after removing the screws or nails. On some designs, the blocks are rabbeted in a large dado or a series of small dadoes. You'll need to pry these out after loosening them. If you have to replace a chair glue block, be sure to cut it so each glue side has grain at a 45° angle for good glue hold.

Once the glue blocks are off, the rest of the chair should come apart easily. Begin by removing the front legs as a single assembly, then remove the seat rails and bottom stretchers. Then, take apart these two assemblies, keeping track of the parts. When all the pieces are apart, check to see what kind of glue was used (See page 29). If it's hide glue, scrape off the large hunks of dried glue and clean out the mortises. Check for broken or damaged joints before regluing, and also be sure to check the fit of the parts. You should be able to fit them together using only moderate hand pressure. If you can wiggle them more than a couple of inches either direction, you'll need to rebuild the wood joints.

To assemble the chair, reverse the disassembly sequence. Do this on a level surface, and have some warm, clean water and rags handy. It's always a good idea to go through a dry clamping run before applying the glue to make sure all the parts fit back together correctly. Using the appropriate glue (See pages 24 to 28), rebuild and clamp the chair in stages. For example, glue together and temporarily clamp the front and back leg sections as separate units, then glue them together. In the case of a "stool" type chair, glue the bottom assembly first, then glue on the top parts. Glue all the separate sections of the chair back together at one time, or you risk getting a section out of square and the chair will wobble.

When the chair is assembled, tighten all the clamps, making sure the chair is on a level surface. If you're not sure if your table is flat, a fairly reliable flat surface is a table saw or a piece of plywood or particleboard. Check the chair for wobbling. If it wobbles, you can force it back into square by skewing the clamps and retightening them until the wobble is gone. You may have to play with several of the clamps before it's gone.

HOW TO DISASSEMBLE A CHAIR FOR REGLUIN

1 Before you begin dismantling the chair, carefully and accurately label each part. Note locations, purposes and any other information that will help you keep the parts straight when it's time to reassemble the chair.

4 To reassemble the chair, divide it into logical working sections. For example, opposing legs and stretchers can be combined into a frame as seen above. Glue up each of these sections, using clamps. Check to make sure the joints are square before the glue sets.

2 Removing the seat and seat board is generally a good place to start. Check for glue blocks under the seat and remove them as well. Pull any fasteners holding the blocks on, then break them loose by striking with a paint scraper or mallet.

3 Carefully disassemble the chair using the techniques discussed in this chapter. In almost all cases, the best plan is to completely disassemble the chair and reglue all of the joints. Once the parts are apart, clean old glue off all the mating ends, using a combination of solvents and scraping with a file or rasp. Getting rid of all the old glue is essential to creating a solid new glue bond.

5 Once the sections are rebuilt and the glue has cured, glue and clamp the sections together to rebuild the entire chair. It's important to glue all sections together at the same time so you can accurately check to make sure the chair is squarely glued and wobble-free.

6 After the glue has cured, reattach the seat using the same attachment methods used in the original construction. NOTE: On some chair types, such as Windsor chairs, the seat is an integral part of the chair structure and should be glued together along with the rest of the parts.

PROBLEM: The split in the top of this small end table occurred because the reinforcing blocking on the underside of the tabletop was screwed in place contiguously across the entire part. This would not allow any cross-grain expansion or contraction to occur, creating internal pressure in the wood that caused the split. Fortunately, a split of this type is not overly difficult to repair using glue and clamps.

Gluing cracks & splits

Cracks and splits are handled differently depending upon whether or not the crack will close under nominal pressure. If it's a recent split or crack due to accidental stress or breakage, it should close easily with hand pressure or very gentle clamping. Gluing the split closed is a relatively easy task. But if the crack or split does not close easily, it probably was created by internal stress in the wood, usually resulting from wood expansion issues. Or, the crack could be from an old break that was repaired improperly. In either of these more difficult cases, there may be splinters from the break rearranged in a manner that's preventing the crack from reclosing. If the crack does not close, check for splinters first. Use a sharp knife to poke around and see if you can pull out any splinters.

If there are no splinters prevent-

HOW TO GLUE TOGETHER A CLEAN CRACK

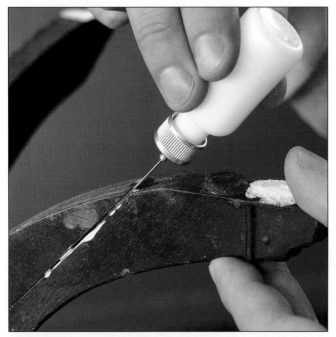

1 If the split or crack closes together neatly with minimal force, gently separate the wood to open up the crack just enough to fit the needle of a glue injector (See page 25) into the crack. Fill the crack with glue.

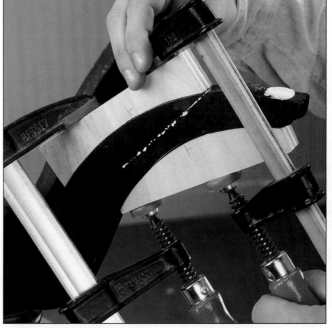

2 Apply gentle clamping pressure on opposite sides of the crack. On contoured parts, like the cabriole leg shown above, you may need to create a clamping block with the reverse profile of the part to even out the clamping pressure. Take care not to apply so much pressure that you force all the glue out of the crack. Some squeeze-out should occur, however. Periodically wipe the repair area with a damp rag to remove the glue.

ing the crack from closing, check for a piece of wood or blocking attached to the cracked part in a cross-grain orientation (See top photo, previous page). If this is the case, what's happening is a flaw in the original design that won't permit shrinkage and expansion of the wood. In this case, you'll not only have to repair the crack, but you'll have to remove the cross-grain piece and reattach it in a way that will allow some wood movement. For example, if the offending cross-grain part or blocking has been glued in place, you can reattach it using only thin brads or wire nails, which will bend enough with the wood movement. Another option is to reglue only a portion of it so the rest can move.

Cracked antiques. Most antique wood furniture was not designed for houses with central heating. Heating cold air and distributing it through an entire house is a relatively recent development, and what this does is to drop the relative humidity to very low levels in the winter. When the relative humidity falls below 10%, furniture that wasn't originally designed to accommodate the resultant shrinkage will crack and split. This is why many fine old antiques made with solid wood sides and tops have cracks and splits. As long as the splits and cracks aren't terribly unsightly, it may be better to leave them. If you repair them, you can cause new problems when the wood expands in the more humid summer months.

Clamping cracks & splits. If the crack or split will close easily, it's a simple matter to repair it. Using clamps, apply pressure in a dry run until you're satisfied that the gap is completely gone. You may have to use several clamps, applying pressure in opposing directions to completely and neatly close the crack. Once you've managed this, remove the clamps and apply glue to both sides of the crack. While there's certainly no harm in using the same glue as was originally used

(most likely hide glue on antiques and PVA glues on modern furniture), a better practice is to use whichever glue gives you the best performance for your specific proj-. ect. As long as it's not a joint that will need to be taken apart later, it's generally an acceptable practice

to use modern glues on antiques with a fresh, clean split or crack. Use a syringe or small piece of wood to get plenty of glue into the crack. Close the clamps back up and wipe the squeeze-out away with a dampened cloth. Set the piece aside to dry, and periodically

HOW TO REPAIR WIDE SPLITS

1 If a crack or split will not close together tightly, or if there is missing wood, you'll need to make a filler strip to fill the gap. Thinner cracks can be filled with strips of wood veneer (See next page). For wider splits, you'll need to cut a slightly wedged filler strip to fit the crack. Cut the strip so it tapers about 5° toward the bottom, which allows you to drive it into the split like a wedge. If you're working on a band saw, tilt the table to about 5°.

2 Clamp the workpiece together to close the split as much as possible. Drive the filler strip you cut into the area of the split where it's needed. Remove and trim the filler if needed. When the fit is correct, you should be able to insert the filler by hand or with only very light tapping. Remove the clamps, glue the filler into the crack as you glue the entire crack, then clamp lightly. Trim the filler with a chisel or hand plane until flush. Touch up the finish (See pages 82 to 83).

wipe away glue, as it will continue to seep out slightly until the glue cures. Remove the clamps.

If the split or crack just won't close completely, you'll have to glue a wedge or small pieces of veneer into the crack to bridge the gap. If the gap is very small, you can usually use strips of veneer as tiny filler pieces. Make sure you orient the veneer in the same direction as the grain in the broken wood. Go through a dry clamping run and see if the veneer shims are snug after the clamps are tightened. If so, apply glue to the crack, insert the veneer and close the clamps. Clean up the excess glue with a toothbrush and some warm water, let the glue cure, then trim the top edge of the veneer flush.

If veneer isn't thick enough to bridge the gap, you'll need to custom-cut a filler piece that will fit snugly into the crack. Find a piece of wood of the same species and color as the project wood. Cut this piece to fit the gap, but cut one edge at a 5° angle. This will wedge it tightly against the crack. Also, you may have to cut the piece to fit the shape of the crack. For example, end splits will taper inward, so you may have to cut a compound taper to get a good fit. Cut the piece by hand or on a band saw with the table tilted to 5°. Once the piece is cut, test-fit it by inserting it into the crack and applying light clamping pressure. Carefully drive the filler piece into the crack and tighten the clamps a bit more. Finesse the fit by driving the piece in as needed or by trimming it to make adjustments in the size and shape. When you're satisfied, remove the filler strip, apply glue, then gently drive the wedge home with a mallet. Tighten the clamps, remove the glue squeeze-out, and let the glue cure. Then, trim the wedge piece using a sharp chisel and fine sandpaper, trying not to disturb the surrounding finish. Touch up the finish on the new wood to blend it in with the old (See pages 82 to 83).

1 Relatively narrow splits in wood that don't quite close up neatly when clamped lightly can be repaired using strips of veneer. First, create a uniform groove for the veneer by running a utility knife through the split. Don't get too aggressive, though, and be sure to use a knife with a very sharp blade. On slightly larger splits or splits that go all the way through the wood, you can use a fine saw blade to clean out a groove.

2 Locate veneer made from the same wood species as your project piece, if possible. Cut the veneer into strips that are slightly wider than the depth of the split. Apply glue to the strips and press them into the gaps in the split.

3 Make sure glue is applied throughout the split or crack, and not just in the area or areas containing filler strips. Once the glue is applied, clamp the split closed. A pipe or bar clamp generally works best. Make sure the jaws of the clamp are padded to protect the edges of the workpiece. Do not overtighten the clamp: this can force out too much glue from the repair and cause the workpiece to contort or cup.

4 After the glue has dried, you can remove the clamps. Wait until the glue has cured, then trim the filler strips so they're flush with the surface of the wood. Use a very sharp wood chisel, beveled edge down, to gently trim the strips. Don't try to take too much material at once; be patient. You can also use the chisel to scrape off any dried glue around the repair area. A sharp hand plane (such as a block plane) may be used instead of a chisel.

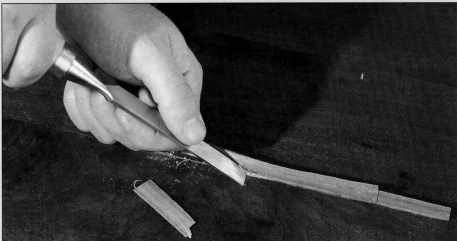

5 Apply pigments with a fine brush to touch up the repair area and surrounding wood as needed. Also blend in new finish over the repair (See pages 82 to 83) and buff the area with fine steel wool to match the original sheen of the finish, if necessary.

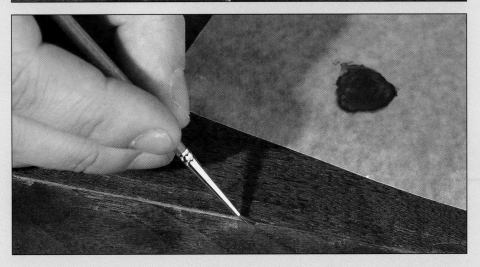

Regluing veneer

Veneer that's loose and raised up or blistered needs to be repaired as quickly as possible. Otherwise, it's easily broken. In addition, the loose area creates an entry point for moisture that can cause the problem to spread.

Blistered veneer is almost always the result of heat or water, or a combination of the two. Both heat and water can soften hide glue (See page 28). Moisture also causes veneer near edges, especially on legs, to split or fray. In some cases, loose veneer is hard to see, so problems can go unnoticed for many years. If you suspect loose veneer, tap the tip of your finger on the suspicious area. Sound veneer will register a "thumping" sound, while areas where the veneer has loosened will resound with a hollow, tapping tone.

With any loose or blistered veneer that's otherwise in good condition, your first repair attempt should always be to apply heat to the area and see if you can stick it back down by reactivating the glue. If the veneer originally was attached with hide glue, there is a fair probability of success. If the veneer isn't split, and the finish is in good shape, you have some chance of reactivating the glue using a household iron (set on medium) and a slightly dampened rag. Lay the rag over the blister and apply the tip of the iron to the rag for a few seconds only. Keep repeating until the veneer lays flat and then clamp it flat (See Tip box, above). If the veneer is split, you can inject some hot water under the veneer. Push down on the damaged area several times to distribute the water and then clamp it when you feel it sticking.

If heat and moisture fail to restick the veneer, you'll need to use fresh glue to do the job. If the loose or blistered area is already split or is at an edge of the furniture, work a palette knife underneath the veneer, through the split or under the edge. Using the knife to

In essence, the bond between veneer and a substrate is a joint and, as such, it needs to be clamped to ensure that the bond is as strong as possible. If the repair area you're working on is near the edge of the workpiece, clamping is greatly simplified. Simply lay a piece of wax paper over the repair, set a rigid board on top of that, then clamp the board over the repair with a couple of pipe clamps, woodscrews or C-clamps (See photo above).

If the veneer repair area is away from the edge and beyond the reach of the clamp throats, you'll need to improvise a bit when it comes to clamping. The easiest thing to do (although not the most effective) is simply to lay wax paper and a board on top of the repair then set a heavy weight, like a stack of encyclopedias, on top of the board. If the workpiece is flat (say, a tabletop that has been removed) make a clamping press from 2 × 4s and plywood, and sandwich the workpiece in the press (See photo, right). A third option is to use the wedge system demonstrated in *Step 3*, on the next page.

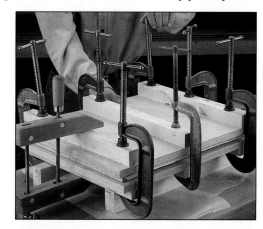

prop open the damaged area, insert some 120-grit sandpaper, grit-side down. Remove the palette knife, then work the sandpaper back and forth to clean out the old glue. Turn the sandpaper over and repeat to clean the underside of the veneer. Blow out the dust, then work some glue under the veneer with the palette knife. Clamp the repair (See Tip box, above). Clean up the squeeze-out with a clean damp rag and an old toothbrush, if necessary.

HOW TO REATTACH LOOSE VENEER

OPTION: Always try reactivating the glue before you get into any more complicated veneer repairs. If the veneer originally was attached with hide glue, it can often be reattached simply by applying heat and moisture to reactivate the glue and renew the bond with the wood. Set a household iron to medium, lay a dampened rag over the damage, and press the iron onto the rag for a few seconds. Try repeating, if necessary. If the veneer sticks, clamp it for awhile. If the veneer still won't stick, move ahead to the following steps.

1 If the veneer has split or is near an edge, work a flexible palette knife under the split (if the blister has not split open, cut through it with a razor knife). Prop the damage area open and work a piece of sandpaper between the veneer and the substrate. Sand the substrate, as well as the underside of the veneer, to remove as much of the old glue as you possibly can. Blow out or vacuum up the dust.

2 Prop open the damaged area with the palette knife again, and inject fresh glue into the area with a glue injector bottle. Press down on the veneer to set it into the glue, wiping up any squeeze-out.

3 Clamp the repair. If working near an edge, simply use pipe or bar clamps and a block (See previous page). If you're working in the field area, where the clamp jaws won't reach, try this trick: Lay a sheet of wax paper over the repair; set a thin, rigid board on top of the paper; attach a bar clamp secure to the workpiece so the bar passes across the center of the repair area; drive wood wedges between the bar and the board to force the board down in a clamp-like fashion.

BEFORE

AFTER

Rehabbing a Rocking Chair

An old rocker stages a comeback for a new generation of young fans.

Even though it was missing a runner, the potential in this kid-size rocking chair was easy to spot. Pressback rockers, sized for children and adults alike, are classic pieces of American furniture. This one was essentially sound from a structural standpoint and the relief detailing on the pressed pine back was in good shape. So we figured that a little work on the band saw making a new runner and a quick strip and finish job were all we'd need to do to ready the rocker for a brand new home. And, amazingly, it turned out we were right.

Before we went too far with any repair work, we took care of a few loose spindle joints (regluing all those joints is likely to change how the parts fit together in the end, which could impact on how the new runner would fit). The joints were loose enough, and the wood was soft enough, that we were able to get enough fresh glue injected into each joint to make a strong bond. If it had been an adult-size chair that would have to stand up to adult-size bodies, we probably would have disassembled the whole thing, cleaned up the spindle ends and then reglued it.

Making the new runner was certainly the trickiest part of this rocker rehab project. Luckily, one

(LEFT) Before we rebuilt the runner for the rocker, we shored up as many joints as we could by injecting glue into them then clamping thoroughly. This tightened up the chair nicely, and because it caused a few of the parts to shift position slightly it was a good thing we did it before we drilled the mounting holes and attached the new runner.

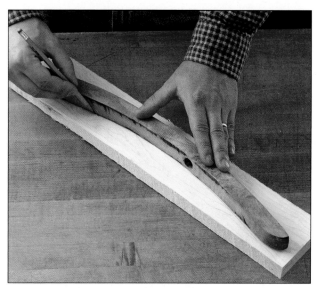

(ABOVE) Using the surviving runner as a template, we outlined the shape for the new runner onto a piece of hard maple. We oriented the outline so the ends of the runner, which are vulnerable to breaking, were composed of long-grain wood, not the fragile short grain.

of the runners was still intact, so we were able to use it as a template for the new one. So we cut the new runner out of maple, smoothed and fitted it, checked and double-checked the fit, then attached it to the rocker leg.

With the chair repaired, we proceeded with the refinishing, using a chemical stripper to remove the old paint. Getting the finish out of the pressback details and the beading in the legs and stringers was a bit of a challenge, but a nutpick and some twine made it go pretty well.

We applied some medium-dark stain to the chair, mostly to help mask the fact that the chair was made of more than one type of wood. But the majority of the wood was fairly soft pine, so we topcoated the chair with three coats of glossy polyurethane varnish, which dried to a hard, slick surface.

~MJ

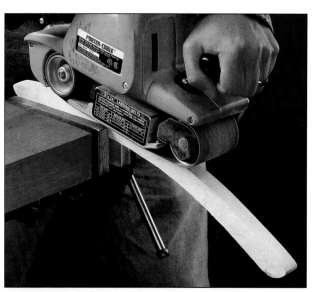

(ABOVE) A few passes with a belt sander and 100-grit belt took care of saw marks and uneven spots on the top and bottom of the new runner. We were especially careful with the bottom edge—any unevenness would be felt every time the chair was rocked.

(LEFT) The replacement runner is clamped to the chair legs so the correct position of the mortises for the round leg ends can be traced onto it. The runner was positioned with the other runner in place and the chair on the floor so we could adjust the new runner as needed until it rocked smoothly. We moved it up to the worksurface to make it easier to lay out the mortise locations.

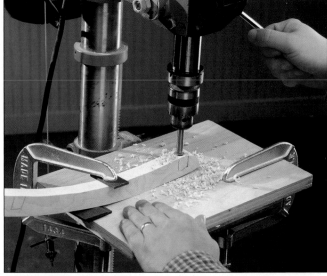

(ABOVE) We clamped the runner to the drill press table then drilled the mortises for the leg ends with a Forstner bit, taking care that the shank of the drill was parallel to the outlines of the legs we'd drawn.

To drill pilot holes for small wire nails or finish nails, snip the head off one of the nails and chuck the cut end into your drill. The nail functions as a perfectly-sized drill bit.

(RIGHT) After dry-fitting both runners onto the chair legs and testing to make sure it rocked smoothly, we glued the runners to the legs and clamped them with bar clamps while the glue set. After the glue was dry, we drilled pilot holes and drove two wire nails into each leg tenon, through the sides of the runners. We countersunk the nails and covered the heads with wood putty.

(RIGHT) The old finish was removed with chemical paint stripper and a variety of scrapers, including nut-picks for getting into the pressback relief areas and baling twine for scouring the shoulders of the beading on the legs and spreaders. We rinsed the entire chair with denatured alcohol to neutralize the stripper. Once it was nice and dry, we hand-sanded all wood surfaces with 100-grit, then 150-grit sandpaper. Because the chair is made of pine, it wasn't necessary to go any finer on the sandpaper. We wiped off the sanding dust with a tack cloth.

(ABOVE) We chose a medium-tone wood stain to color the chair. The stain was just dark enough to conceal the fact that the runners and the the chair body were made from different wood species. Then we topcoated it with three thin coats of gloss polyurethane varnish for a hard, slick surface that's durable, easy to clean and resistance-free for sliding onto the seat.

Skills used in this project:

• *Regluing mortise-and-tenon joints (pages 52 to 53)*

• *Making replacement parts (pages 56 to 59)*

• *Removing a finish (pages 100 to 111)*

• *Sanding (pages 118 to 121)*

• *Applying a finish (pages 128 to 155)*

Graft new wood onto the workpiece to replace missing wood, then shape the new wood to match the contours and profiles of the part. Make sure the surfaces on the part where the wood is missing are clean and square, then glue and clamp an oversized chunk of replacement wood into the damage area—see the square chunk of red oak glued to the pedestal leg above. Once the new wood is secured, trim it to rough size with a hand saw, then shape and carve it as needed to match, using chisels and files. The same general idea is used to repair missing corners (See page 68).

Repairing Wood Joints & Parts

This chapter discusses techniques for replacing wood that's too damaged to reglue, wood that's missing, or wood that's worn and rotted. When it comes to replacing wood, there's one very simple rule you'll do well to follow: Always replace wood with wood. It's often tempting to take the quick and easy route and stuff a little plaster, wax or putty into a structural crack, or use it to rebuild crushed corners or build up caster holes. While these products are perfectly okay to use for making repairs to small dents, gouges and other minor problems, they don't work as well as real wood when it comes to repairing or replacing large sections of wood. Not only do they eventually fail, they don't age in accord with the rest of the wood, becoming more and more conspicuous over time.

Replacing wood is necessary in certain situations for proper regluing of loose furniture joints. Joints may also weaken from accidental stress or shock, loosening the joint so that normal everyday use may break it. In the case of rebuilding joints, you may want to review the strategies for dismantling (See pages 35 to 39). Removing the joint that's damaged makes it easier to work on it, and it also provides complete access to the entire joint surface.

One of the most common places for wood deterioration or loss to occur is around fasteners. The most obvious problem this creates is that the fasteners loosen or fail. There are a host of tricks you'll run into for beefing up the hole so it will hold a new fastener (drive a golf tee into the old hole; fill the hole with

A plug cutter mounts in your drill press and can be used to cut wood plugs for making furniture repairs and filling counterbores.

toothpicks and glue. . . everyone seems to have a personal favorite). Many of the fixes can provide short-term solutions, but sooner or later they're likely to fail too. For a more permanent (and more professional-looking) solution, replace the stripped area with solid, new wood. First, pick a Forstner bit of the appropriate diameter to drill a hole to remove the area around the damaged wood. Keep clear of the edges of the wood as much as you can. If you have a problem trying to get the hole started because the center spur on the bit has nothing hard to contact, guide the bit by drilling through a piece of hardwood with the same drill bit to make a drill "guide." Clamp the guide to the workpiece so the hole is directly above the damaged area and use it as a guide to start the drill. It's a good idea to put a piece of tape on the shank of the drill bit to let you know when you've drilled to the depth you want. Plug the hole with a dowel, oriented with the grain running in the same direction as the workpiece. If the plug will be in a visible area, mount a plug cutter in your drill press and cut a plug from the same species of wood as the workpiece (or, in some cases, you might consider mining a plug for a visible area from a hard-to-see spot, then filling the hole in the less visible spot with new wood that may not be a perfect match).

A Note on Dovetails

Dovetails are classic furnituremaking joints that form strong, mechanical locks. These joints are incredibly strong and the only time you're likely to encounter problems with them are in very high stress areas, such as drawer boxes. As with any other failed joint, try the simplest solution first: reglue and clamp the joint. If you have a dovetail joint with broken pins, disassemble the joint, then trim the broken pin if needed to create a square line at the base of the pin. Use the surrounding pins as a guide for manufacturing a replacement pin. Cut it slightly overlong. Reassemble and glue the joint, then glue the replacement pin in the appropriate tail slot. Once the glue sets, trim the new pin until it fits perfectly by paring the sides with a sharp chisel.

HOW TO REPAIR A STRIPPED SCREW HOLE

1 Remove the metal fastener, using a screw extractor if necessary (See page 19). Use a Forstner bit slightly larger than the affected area's diameter (but not so large it removes wood too close to the edges) and drill out the damage, using a drilling guide if needed. Make the guide by drilling a straight hole through a piece of hardwood to align over the center of the drilling area.

2 Cut a piece of doweling the same diameter as the hole (or use a plug cutter to make a wood plug—see photo, left). Apply glue to the plug and drive it into the hole. The exposed end should project slightly above the surface.

3 After the glue sets, file the end of the plug down until it is flush with the surrounding surface. If the surface is curved, as shown above, use a round file. Clean up the surface by sanding, if necessary.

BUILDING-UP A TENON

1 Loose mortise-and-tenon joints generally mean that the tenons are too small, either from shrinkage or sloppy work in the original construction. The easiest solution to this problem is to enlarge, or build up, the tenon. Start by disassembling the joint and cleaning the old glue from the mating parts with a chisel, file, scraper or sandpaper.

2 Cut strips of wood veneer (try to find the same species as the part) and glue a piece to each broad "cheek" of the tenon. The pieces should be slightly oversized. You'll get a better glue bond if you cut small clamp pads to distribute clamping pressure over the cheeks as the glue dries (slip a piece of wax paper between the pads and veneer to prevent bonding with the pads).

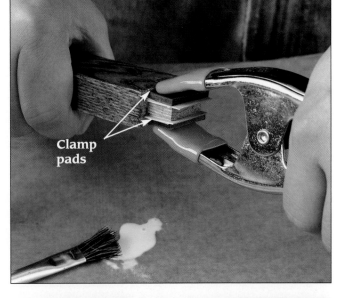

Clamp pads

3 File or plane the tenon as needed to reduce it so it fits snugly into the mortise, using only hand pressure. Once the fit is good, glue the joint together and clamp until the glue is dry.

Mortise-and-tenon joints

Mortise-and-tenon joints are a preferred means of reinforcing glue joints in fine furnituremaking, although they're seldom used in modern production-style furnishings. They are composed of a tenon, which can be round or rectangular, that's shaped into the end of one of the mating boards. The other board contains the mortise—a hole shaped and sized to accept the tenon.

Because the tenon is hidden when the joint is assembled, it's not always easy to identify the joint until it is broken or disassembled. In some cases, however, the mortise runs all the way through the joint, exposing the end of the tenon—called a *through mortise.* Mortise-and-tenon joints often are pinned with dowels that run through the joint in a perpendicular direction. Through mortise-and-tenon joints can be pinned or secured with small wedges driven into the end of the tenon.

Mortises that are cracked or split can be reglued as long as the wood closes snugly so the glue will stick. If not, a new piece of wood should be spliced into the joint and the mortise resized to accept the enlarged tenon. If the joint is broken, damaged or rotted, you'll need to clean out the mortise by drilling with a Forstner bit. This is best

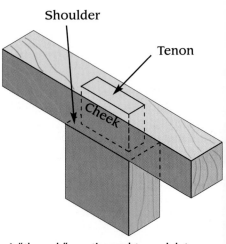

Shoulder

Tenon

Cheek

A "through" mortise-and-tenon joint

done on a drill press. You can also do this with a router bit, provided you use a bearing guided bit and a template to guide it.

Building up tenons. If a mortise-and-tenon joint doesn't make good wood-to-wood contact when reglued, or if you had to scrape away a lot of wood to remove glue, you need to build up the cheeks of the tenon to get a good fit. Before starting, make sure the mortise walls are clean. To beef up a small tenon, glue a piece of veneer, cut slightly oversized, to each broad tenon cheek—it's important to add wood to both opposing cheeks to preserve the offset of the joint. When the glue has dried, trim the excess veneer and check the fit. The tenon will probably be too tight. But if it's still loose, glue on two more pieces of veneer. Once the tenon is larger than the mortise, trim back the tenon cheeks with a wood plane, rasp or sandpaper. Remove just a little of the wood at a time. When the fit is correct, you'll be able to push the tenon into the mortise with only gentle hand pressure.

TIP: Round tenons can be enlarged to fit into oversized mortise holes by either wrapping the tenon in a glue-soaked plane shaving or by expanding the tenon diameter with a wedge.

Fixing broken tenons. Occasionally, a tenon breaks off in the mortise. This can occur with either round or rectangular joints. If this happens, you'll need to disassemble the parts, then drill out the old tenon from the old mortise. Also trim any remaining wood from the tenon at the shoulder of the tenoned piece. Next, cut a mortise that's the same size as the original mortise into the cut end of the tenoned piece. Now, simply make a spline that's twice the length of the original tenon. Reassemble and glue the joint so half of the spline is seated in each mating part. Be sure to test the fit of the spline before gluing, and trim as needed.

HOW TO REPLACE A BROKEN TENON

1 Disassemble the joint, then cut off any remaining chunks or splinters of the tenon from the tenoned part so the end is smooth. Secure the workpiece in a padded vise. Use a flush-cutting saw to do the trimming.

2 Remove the remains of the old tenon from the mortise by drilling a series of holes into the tenon, using a drill bit the same diameter as the width of the original tenon. On round tenons, you can remove all the waste with one hole if you select a Forstner bit of the same diameter as the tenon. Be sure to clamp the workpiece securely to prevent it from splitting. Clean up the edges of the mortise with a sharp chisel, if necessary.

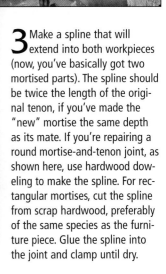

3 Make a spline that will extend into both workpieces (now, you've basically got two mortised parts). The spline should be twice the length of the original tenon, if you've made the "new" mortise the same depth as its mate. If you're repairing a round mortise-and-tenon joint, as shown here, use hardwood doweling to make the spline. For rectangular mortises, cut the spline from scrap hardwood, preferably of the same species as the furniture piece. Glue the spline into the joint and clamp until dry.

1 Disassemble the joint, then cut off the chunks and splinters of the broken dowel from both mating parts, using a flush-cutting saw.

2 Install a brad-point or Forstner bit ¹⁄₁₆ in. smaller in diameter than the old dowels, then drill out the old dowels, doing your best not to let the drill wander into the wood.

Dowel joints

Since the mid 1850s dowels have been used as replacements for the mortise-and-tenon, dovetail and other traditional joints. Though despised by purists, proper doweling creates a very strong and durable joint. Like any other joint, stresses and contrary wood movement will invariably loosen the dowel in at least one of the components. When this occurs, the dowel should be reglued or replaced.

Dowel joints are made with a variety of orientations and, like mortise-and-tenon joints, some of them are hard to detect without disassembling the joint. Almost all dowel reinforcements are hidden, however.

Many times, a dowel will simply loosen when the grain of the dowel is at a right angle to the grain of the component. The joint can be tapped apart with a soft-faced mallet and then reglued. Other times, the dowel will break and the old dowel must be drilled out and replaced. If the new dowel does not seat exactly like the old one, misalignment of the joint will result.

Replacing a dowel. Begin by cutting the dowel flush to the surface of the component with a sharp saw. Using a sharp brad-point or Forstner bit around ¹⁄₁₆ in. smaller than the diameter of the dowel, drill out the center of the dowel. Hold the part in a padded vise. When the bit reaches the bottom of the dowel hole, you will feel the bit "slip" a bit and you can stop. Using a sharp gouge with a sweep that matches the curve of the dowel circumference (See page 14), pare the excess dowel away from the sides of the hole. To clean the hole, run a drill bit of the correct diameter into the hole with the drill set to reverse (the bit can catch and rip the hole apart if run forward).

Don't use new dowels to check the fit. These can seize in the joint and become difficult to remove. Use dowels that have been pared or sanded so they're slightly undersized. These are easier to remove after a trial fit.

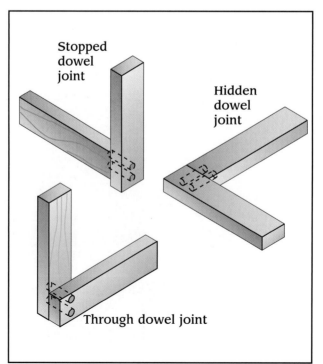

Stopped dowel joint

Hidden dowel joint

Through dowel joint

3 Use a curved gouge to carefully pare away the remaining wood of the old dowels. Don't get carried away: if the new dowel hole you're making is slightly too large or offset from the old hole, the parts will not fit together properly. See page 14 for information on choosing a gouge that will work for your project.

Run drill in reverse when cleaning out dowel holes

4 Switch to a brad-point or Forstner bit that matches the dowel diameter exactly, and use it to clean out the edges of the dowel holes. To be on the safe side, run your drill in reverse so it doesn't engage the wood and deepen or widen the hole.

5 Test the fit of the replacement dowel (use woodworkers' dowel pins, not lengths of regular doweling, whenever possible). To be on the safe side, sand the dowel down slightly before inserting it— you don't want it to fit so tightly that you cause damage when you pull it out. If the fit is still tight, continue to pare back the dowel, but don't widen the hole. Once you get the correct fit, glue and clamp the joint.

Repairing & replacing wood parts

Furniture breaks. No matter how careful you are or how well made the furnishings, accidents and wear will take their toll eventually. Legs, arms, stretchers and other wooden parts will splinter or snap, especially as the wood becomes increasingly drier with age. Simple fractures where no wood is lost can be glued together if the break is clean. But as with joints, if a wood part needs repair or replacement, your best bet is to replace it with new wood.

With-the-grain breaks. If a wood part breaks or splinters and the break runs with, or very close to, the direction of the grain, the best thing to do is just reglue it. As long as you can put the wooden parts together with no visible gaps, the glue will create a bond stronger than the wood itself. If the joints don't close easily, look at the parts and see if there are any splinters that are bent or broken and may be preventing the parts from closing. You may need to trim them or break them off to get a good fit. You should be able to push the joints together tightly with a little pressure. As long at the wood is clean and the parts fit well, there's no need to reinforce the joint with mechanical fasteners or dowels.

Cross-grain breaks. When a break is against the grain of the part, or at a right angle to the grain, it can't be repaired with simple regluing. End grain will not bond to end grain unless some sort of reinforcement is used. The parts that suffer most frequently

REPAIRING A CROSS-GRAIN BREAK

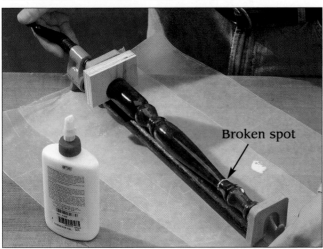

1 Carefully glue the broken part back together, doing your best to eliminate any gaps and get a good clean fit. Fit the part into a bar or pipe clamp. You may need to clamp around the break, as well. Let the glue set before removing the clamps.

2 Find a low-visibility spot along the break and wrap a piece of masking tape around it. Draw a registration line across the tape, then mark a cutting line. Cut through the leg, sawing at a right angle. Make multiple thin cuts all around the part, using a thin-kerf saw.

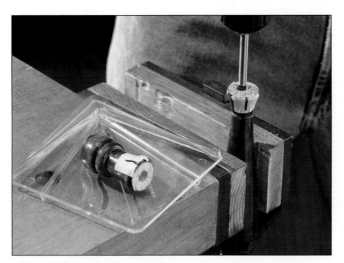

3 Use a centerfinder to locate the center of each cut end. Drill a dowel hole, at least 1½ in. deep, in each part at the centerpoint. Take care to keep the drill vertical and aligned with the part.

4 Cut a dowel rod slightly shorter than the combined depth of the two holes. The rod should be the same diameter as the holes. Cut grooves in the dowel so excess glue can squeeze out. Dry-fit the parts and adjust as needed. Glue and clamp the parts together, lining them up with the registration line. Touch up the joint after the glue sets.

from cross-grain breaks are turned legs—the narrower sections of the part create natural weak spots. To properly repair a break of this type you'll need to use reinforcement along with glue. This is easy to do if the break is close to the end. Just reglue the break, making sure you align the pieces correctly. Apply glue to both parts and use a bar clamp to clamp them together. Make sure the part is straight, checking it from several angles to make sure. When the glue is dry, remove the clamp and mark the center with a center finder (if there is a dimple in the end of the part from the lathe center, you can use this as a starting mark). Find the thinnest area of the part, within and slightly beyond the broken area, and choose a drill bit that's at least half that thickness. Drill a hole at the centerpoint, at least an inch beyond the broken area, making sure you keep the drill straight (it's not a bad idea to have a friend watch from the side and tell you if you're veering off vertical). Clean out the hole, then cut a dowel pin from dowel rod that's the same diameter as the hole. Cut grooves in the dowel with a dovetail saw so the glue can escape, then glue the dowel into the dowel hole, seating it with a few taps from a wooden mallet. Trim the end flush when the glue dries.

If the break is in the middle of a leg, or far enough so a drill bit can't reach it, you'll have to do the repair differently. Glue the broken leg back together in a bar or pipe clamp. When it's dry, find an inconspicuous spot in the damaged area, like the top of a turned ball, where you can cut the part cleanly in half. Make small marks above and below the cutting line so you can register the pieces later. Cut the part in two, following the cutting lines. Rather than starting and cutting all the way through, start sawing to a depth of ⅛ in. then move to another area. Saw "round and round" until you get through. Mark the centers of each cut end with a center finder and drill straight, vertical holes at least 1½ in. into each part with a drill bit at least half the diameter of the part. Insert a dowel into the parts and check the fit, using the marks you made earlier to align the pieces. When satisfied, take it apart and reassemble using glue.

If a leg or some other part is broken in more than one place, it may be best to replace the whole part. If you have the equipment and experience, make the part yourself. Otherwise, have it made for you.

Making new wood parts

Manufacturing a new wood part to replace one that's broken beyond repair takes a bit of imagination and perhaps a little courage. But if you have a decent selection of tools and some basic woodworking knowledge, there's no reason you can't manage it successfully. Here are a few pointers to keep in mind:

• Use the original part (or an identical part from elsewhere in the piece) as a template whenever possible.

• Don't skimp on the wood: the best results will be obtained from the same wood species, even if you're planning to paint the piece.

• Always err on the side of making the part too big. It's easy to pare it down to size, but next to impossible to make it bigger.

• The photos at right are from a rocker repair sequence you'll find on pages 46 to 49.

"New parts" aren't limited to legs, spindles and stringers. Tabletops take a disproportionate amount of abuse, compared to the undercarriage parts. And broad panels tend to have many more warping and wood movement problems. In the photo above, a new trunk lid is being made to replace the missing lid on an antique trunk. See pages 84 to 87.

Repairing drawer runners. One of the most common areas where you have to replace wood is on worn drawer sides. Wooden drawers and the runners that guide them wear out over time due to friction. You can usually tell when a drawer needs attention because it no longer operates smoothly. It may scrape badly when you push it in, or it may tip downward. It may rack from uneven pulling pressure or it may just stick badly.

First of all, determine what you need to do by removing the drawer. Examine the drawer runners, which are the wooden supports that guide the drawer as it is used. If they are deeply grooved and worn, you'll need to replace them. Hopefully, you have a design which allows you to turn them over (as in the case when they are flat and simply screwed to the cabinet sides). If not, remove the best one you have and use it as a template to make new runners.

Now, put the drawer back in and see how it works. If it still doesn't operate smoothly, you'll need to build up the bottom of the drawer side that rides on the runners. In most cases, the sides will be worn at an angle. You can check, by holding a large carpenter's square on the drawer and using the front of the drawer to register one side. If there's a large gap between the top of the square and the bottom of the drawer, you'll have to replace it with new wood.

Hold the square so the outside edge of one side is flush with the face of the drawer. Move the square up until you can mark a pencil line on good wood down to the back of the drawer. If you can remove the drawer side, you can cut up to the pencil line with a table saw. If you want to leave the side on, use a portable circular saw or a hand saw. If the bottom of the drawer is exposed, you'll have to remove the side so you can cut it by hand. Plane the wood flush and straight with a small plane and glue on a piece of new wood that's slightly oversized. It should extend just below the bottom of the drawer front and be slightly thicker than the side of the drawer. Glue it on. When the glue dries, trim it with a plane so it's flush to the bottom of the drawer front, and it's the same thickness as the original side. The drawer should now work fine, but check it for fit and operation, and remove more wood from the bottom if it's too tight.

HOW TO REPAIR A DRAWER RUNNER

1 To repair a worn drawer runner, begin by using a carpenter's square as a straight-edge for drawing a cutting line just above the highest worn area on the drawer. The line should be square to the front and back of the drawer.

2 Cut off the old runner, sawing along the cutting line. If you've disassembled the drawer you can make the cut on a table saw. Otherwise, use a hand saw or a circular saw with a cutting guide clamped to the drawer.

3 Cut a replacement runner. When attached, the bottom of the runner should extend past the bottoms of the other drawer parts slightly. Clamp and glue the replacement runner in position.

4 After the glue has set, test the fit of the drawer in the drawer opening. Use a hand plane to trim the new runner down until the drawer rides level and operates smoothly.

5 Stain the new part to age it slightly so it blends in with the rest of the drawer box. You can also apply a coat of paste wax to the runners to make them operate more smoothly and with less resistance, extending their life.

Making scarf joints

The scarf joint is a highly useful method for re-attaching parts that have split off on a diagonal or for creating more gluing surface to get a better bond when attaching narrow wood parts, like tenons—especially if there is not enough "meat" below the shoulder to accept a dowel of the same diameter as the tenon hole (as shown in *How to replace a broken tenon,* page 53).

The basic principle with a scarf joint is that wood glues best when it's glued on the "long grain," usually at an angle of 30° or less. Since end grain will not bond to end grain, the low angle of this joint allows enough long grain so the wood will bond.

To repair a spindle or a chair stretcher with a tenon on the end, cut off the tenon end below the shoulder at an angle of 30° or less. Clean up the saw marks with a sanding board. Hold a piece of oversized wood that's matched for species and grain direction behind it and mark the angle with a pencil. Cut this with a saw and clean up the saw marks. Flatten the wood with a sanding board. Glue on the oversized piece and when dry, trim and smooth it with sandpaper.

To use a scarf joint to replace or reattach a part that has broken off on the diagonal, follow the steps shown below.

HOW TO ATTACH A NEW WOOD PART USING A SCARF JOINT

1 In the project shown above, the end of one of the pedestal table feet broke off and was lost. The break was clean so it was not necessary to make a straight cut above the break line. To make the replacement part, obtain a piece of wood of the same species and thickness as the missing part. Use a similar part as a template, orienting the new wood so the grain lines run in the same direction as the grain near the damaged area.

2 Cut out the new part, using a band saw or scroll saw. Make the part slightly oversized and long so it can be trimmed to an exact fit. Position the cut part in the area where it will be attached and mark a cutting line along the scarf line. Make the cut.

3 Clamp and glue the new part in place. In the photo above, a spring clamp with adjustable miter jaws is used to steady the new part while the glue dries.

4 Clean up any dried glue squeeze-out with a chisel, then shape and contour the part to blend in with its surroundings. Here, a wood chisel and gouges are used to extend the beading.

Repairing veneer

When veneer is broken and missing, you'll have to cut a new piece and glue it in. If the veneer is intact but blistered or loose, see pages 44 to 45. There are several things to keep in mind when replacing veneer.

• Never cut a new piece with an edge that's perpendicular to the original grain (unless, of course, it's part of the original design). This makes the patch piece very visible. Instead, make angled cuts to splice in the new piece, which results in a less visible patch.

• Match the new piece primarily by grain and texture. These two guidelines are more important than color. Color can always be tweaked, but grain and texture are hard to fake. And always make the new piece from a lighter color veneer, not a darker one.

• The replacement veneer should be thicker than the old veneer so you can sand it flush. If the new veneer is too thin (which is often the case with very old veneer), you can use solid wood that's cut to the thickness you need or simply glue two sheets of veneer together to make a new piece.

• It's best if you have several large pieces of veneer to choose your patch from. That way, you can pick from an area that has the best grain, figure and color to blend in with the original.

Removing old veneer. Sometimes veneer is so damaged that it's better to replace all the veneer than try to patch it. Obviously, you'll need to remove the old veneer and prepare the original substrate so the new veneer will stick. To remove old veneer, wet an old towel with hot water and wring out most of the excess water. Lay it over the veneer and let it sit for 30 minutes. Lift it up and see if the veneer has loosened at all by prying up a corner with a putty knife. If it hasn't, re-wet the towel and put it back down and check it every 30 to 60 minutes to see if the glue

HOW TO REMOVE OLD VENEER

1 If the veneered surface has a finish, strip it off so moisture can penetrate through the veneer and into the adhesive. Then, soak a clean towel in water and lay it over the veneered surface, letting the moisture work its way in. Check after a half hour or so to see if there has been any loosening of the veneer. Re-moisten the towel and repeat as necessary.

2 Once the veneer has started to loosen, use a household iron to accelerate the process. Set the iron to medium and pass it back and forth across the towel. Have scraping tools handy so you can attempt to remove the veneer before the adhesive cools and rehardens.

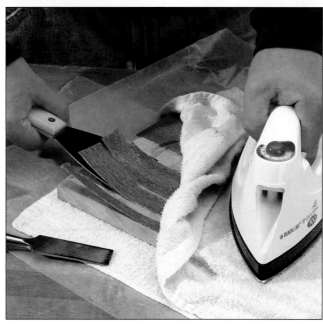

3 Use a combination of scraping tools, including putty knives and chisels, to work the veneer loose and remove it from the surface. Reheat the surface with the iron, just ahead of the place where you're working. Once all (or nearly all) of the veneer has been removed, let the substrate dry, then sand off the adhesive residue with 100-grit sandpaper. Be sure to wipe the substrate clean with a rag and mineral spirits before applying new veneer.

has softened and the veneer can be pried up. When you can pry up the veneer, set a household iron to medium and lay it over the towel. Let it sit for 10 seconds, then move it so you can slip a putty knife underneath it. The veneer should come up easily. Keep heating and prying until all of the veneer has been removed. When the surface has dried, scrape or chisel off any small bits of old veneer. Then, sand the surface with 100-grit paper, right down to bare wood. Make sure you get all the glue off and expose fresh wood.

Replacing large sections of veneer. The easiest method for replacing veneer in large sections, without a lot of complicated presses and veneering equipment, is with paper-backed veneer and contact cement, or with veneer that has heat-sensitive glue already applied. Look for a sheet that's oversized for the replacement area, as you'll trim it after it's glued down. Apply contact cement to both surfaces, following the directions on the can. You may need several coats on the substrate.

Attaching the veneer is a bit like attaching plastic laminate to a countertop. Lay several long strips of wood or doweling on the glued substrate, and position the veneer so it overhangs the edges. Remove one of the wood strips near an edge and press down on the veneer. Remove the strip next to it and continue pressing down so you lay down the veneer in a smooth motion without bubbles. You only get one chance at this with contact cement, so get it right the first time. If you make a mistake, you'll have to start over completely, which means cleaning off the glue, sanding and starting with a new piece of veneer. Once the veneer is down and flat, with no bubbles, use a rubber J-roller to set the veneer into the adhesive. Start in the center and work toward the edges. When the glue has dried, trim off the excess.

Replacing veneer near an edge. To replace veneer near an edge, an adjustable protractor is used for transferring angles (you want to avoid straight, perpendicular cuts). You can use a metal straightedge as a cutting guide, but it may take some trial-and-error, which is likely to create waste as you make multiple cuts to get a precise fit. To start, mark cutting lines around the missing section, angling out toward the edge. Make sure the lines intersect at a point above the damaged or missing area. Lay the protractor head up against the edge, swing the arm up to one of the lines and lock it down. Using a craft knife with a new blade, make a cut with a slight inward bevel, cutting toward

HOW REPAIR VENEER AT A SURFACE EDGE

1 Use a protractor with a locking head as a cutting guide for scoring clean lines around the damaged areas. Set the angle of the protractor so it creates a line tangent to the veneer grain (never cut perpendicular to the grain). Holding a craft knife at a slight bevel (the cutting line should slope away from the middle of the damage area) slice through the veneer to create a triangular outline around the damage.

5 Brush a thin coat of glue onto the back of the veneer patch. We used white PVA glue, even though it lubricates the patch and can cause it to slip out of position when clamped (See step 6). Another option is to use a thin coat of fast-setting cyano-acrylate glue (super glue), which requires no clamping, allowing you to see the patch and get it positioned just right.

2 Without changing the setting of the head, cut a triangular veneer patch from new material, using the protractor as a guide. Bevel the cuts so the edges slope toward the middle of the patch. The patch should be longer than the repair area, with the grain parallel to the workpiece grain.

3 Use a sharp wood chisel to scrape old veneer remnants from the substrate in the repair area. Clean up the cut edges with sandpaper. Also sand the substrate to remove adhesive residue.

4 Test-fit the veneer patch into the repair opening. If the patch is too wide, trim it down on a sanding board—avoid trimming or altering the old veneer at the edges of the repair opening.

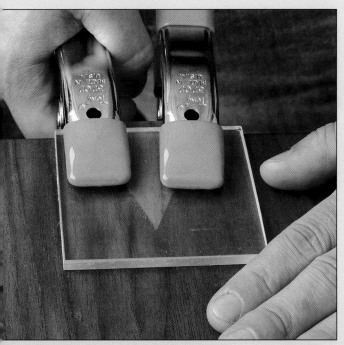

6 Clamp the patch in place. In order to see if the patch is correctly positioned, we used a small piece of clear plexiglas as a clamping pad. Held in place with spring clamps, the pad will not bond with the glue. It will allow slight adjustments to be made to the patch position by tapping on the clamps or pad.

7 Once the glue has set, remove the clamps and use a straightedge and craft knife to trim the end of the veneer flush with the edge of the board. Sand the patch with a sanding block and fine sandpaper until the surface of the patch is level with the surrounding surfaces.

1 Cut out the damaged veneer. You'll need fresh, clean lines to get a good repair. A craft knife following a straightedge works well for cutting. Remove the old material so you leave behind a non-square area with no cutting lines perpendicular to the wood grain.

2 Carefully pry out the splinters of old veneer from the repair area. A sharp chisel is a good tool for this. All the edges should be nice and straight. If not, re-cut them or sand them lightly with a sanding block.

the edge. Use the arm of the protractor as a cutting guide. This cuts the old veneer out at an angle, resulting in a cleaner seam when you glue in the new material. Now, lay the protractor (set at the same angle) over the replacement piece. This time when you make your cut, hold the knife at the opposite bevel. Repeat the process for the other cut on the old veneer, repositioning the arm of the protractor, if necessary. Make the same beveled cuts as you did for the other side. Clean out the sides of the cuts you made on the old veneer with a sharp chisel, if necessary.

You should now have a wedge-shaped piece that will fit seamlessly into the old veneer. If you have to make any adjustments, it's best to use a sanding board. The only step left is to glue the new patch in place. The problem is that when you clamp veneer wedges, the glue acts as a lubricant, which causes the piece to shift slightly out of position. There are two ways around this problem: 1) Use a small piece of plexiglas as a caul. You'll see the piece shift under the clamp and you can tap on the edge of the caul or the clamp to tap it back into posi-

tion; 2) Use a fast-setting cyano-acrylate (super) glue. Apply medium or thick viscosity cyano-acrylate to the veneer; spread thinly. Apply accelerator to the excavated hole. Place the veneer into position and immediately press down on it using a piece of melamine or waxed wood.

Replacing veneer in the middle. When veneer needs to be replaced away from an edge, the easiest way to replace it is to cut out the damage in a diamond or irregular shape, following the natural grain of the veneer if possible. You can use a craft knife, or rout out the shape freehand with a router. Lay a piece of typing or copy paper over the area you removed and rub the flat edge of a pencil across the paper to transfer the outline of the shape to the paper. Glue the paper to your new veneer with temporary or spray contact adhesive. With your craft knife, cut out the veneer patch slightly oversize, following the outside of the edge delineated by the rubbing. Then, remove the paper and glue in the patch using a deep-throated clamp from the edge or long bar clamps and wedges (See pages 44 to 45).

Veneering curves

Repairing damaged veneer on a curved surface can be tricky, but there are strategies for dealing with this challenging repair. If you curve the veneer prior to gluing, it will follow the contour more easily. Using pieces of thin wood as "rulers," cut away the veneer section you need to replace and cut a new piece to fit. Then, soak the veneer in water. Let it dry. It will naturally curl in one direction, making it easier to glue in. To glue it, you can use fast-setting super glue. If you cannot use super glue (as in period furniture), small sandbags can be made which will conform to the shape of the curve and hold the veneer in place while the PVA or hide glue sets.

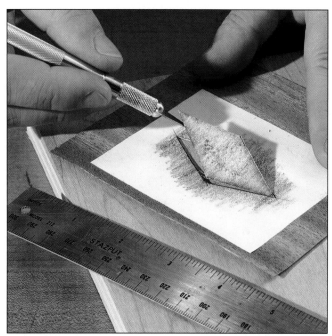

3 Tape a piece of paper over the repair area and shade around the edges with a soft pencil, making a rubbing of the outline. Work to get a clear, dark line at the edges. Take care removing the tape, and wipe off any adhesive left behind right away.

4 Attach the rubbing face-up to the patch material, using spray adhesive. Make sure the rubbing is oriented in the same manner to the grain of the new veneer as it was to the old. Carefully cut through both the rubbing and the patching veneer with your craft knife. It's better to cut slightly outside the lines and trim later than to try and get a perfect fit on the first cut, only to end up with a patch that's too small. Peel the paper off the veneer and remove leftover adhesive.

5 Test the fit of the patch. Make any necessary adjustments by rubbing the edges of the patch on a sanding board with 100-grit sandpaper. Take only a little material at a time, working until the fit is exactly perfect.

6 Glue the patch into the repair area with PVA glue or hide glue. To clamp it down, press a piece of clear plexiglas over the patch. If you don't have the pipe clamp accessory shown here, you can rig up a few wedges to apply the pressure (See page 45). If using a clamp board that will bond with glue, be sure to slip some wax paper between it and the patch. Clean up glue squeeze-out after you remove the clamp.

1 Use mineral spirits to thoroughly clean the original appliqué or molding you intend to reproduce. In many cases, you won't even need to remove it from the piece of furniture.

2 Purchase some two-part casting compound from your local art supply store or a specialty furniture restoration catalog. The product shown above, called "Silputty," was obtained through a restoration catalog (See list of manufacturers, page 160). Knead equal parts of the casting material together, following the product instructions.

Casting replacement parts

Decorative moldings break or simply fall off and disappear, leaving behind only a shadow on the finish that detracts from the appearance of the furnishing. And as often as not, finding a replacement piece that matches exactly is next to impossible. You may have better luck locating bits or cutters that come close to matching so you can shape a new piece from wood. But these bits tend to be costly and require fairly advanced woodworking skills to get good results. It's in scenarios such as this where violating the prime furniture repair directive, "Replace wood with wood," might make sense. If there is an identical appliqué or decorative molding still intact on the piece, you can use it to form a mold for casting a new piece with wood repair compound or even fiberglass filler.

The mold you'll need to make is formed with two-part flexible casting compound, available through art and hobby stores and some wood restoration catalogs. The compound is blended and kneaded together, then pressed over the part you're trying to match to make the mold. After the material sets, it can be pulled off and used to cast impressions of the original. For casting material, you can use two-part polyester wood restorer (*Minwax* makes one) or, in some cases, plaster of Paris or even water putty (like *Durham's* water putty). Pour or press the casting material into the mold, let it dry, and bend back the mold to remove the casting. Make as many impressions as you need. When the cast part is dry, you can color it to match the original furniture or paint it.

OPTION: Use a scratch stock and custom-honed cutter blade to re-create decorative moldings and trim. The cutter is made by tracing a reverse profile of the missing section of molding onto a piece of scrap metal. Then, the cutter is secured into the scratch stock and scraped over the edge of a piece of matching wood to carve the desired profile. See pages 20 to 21 for more information on making and using a scratch stock.

3 Form the kneaded casting compound into a ball and press it onto the item being reproduced. Press firmly to make sure you get an accurate impression. Allow the compound to dry and set up according to the manufacturer's directions (around 5 to 10 minutes for the product shown here). Remove the compound and inspect the impression to make sure it meets with your satisfaction.

4 Prepare a mixture of wood filler compound, plaster of Paris or wood putty (fiberglass filler product, such as the *Minwax* product shown here or even *Bondo* auto body filler product is more durable than plaster or putty). Press or pour the mixture into the mold. Strike off the excess across the top of the mold to create a smooth back for the cast part. Let the material dry for the length of time specified by the manufacturer.

5 Remove the new part from the mold. Use a razor knife and sandpaper to clean up any rough edges. Paint or finish the new part to match the others, then attach it to the furnishing with glue, taking care not to damage it.

1 Cut off the corner at a diagonal angle (less than 30°) to create a clean, straight bonding surface for the replacement wood. Use a straightedge to guide your saw to help ensure that the cut is straight.

2 Smooth out the cut edge with a hand plane and sandpaper so the wood is absolutely level and smooth (this is a similar process to jointing the edges of boards before edge-gluing them to form a panel).

3 Cut a wood patch from wood of the same species. Cut a larger blank first, then position the blank behind the board being repaired, orienting the patch so the grain is parallel to the grain on the workpiece. Draw cutting lines on the patch, extending the edges of the workpiece. Cut the patch oversized, with a smooth, straight edge for the joint. Attach it to the workpiece with glue and clamps. After the glue dries, trim and shape the patch to fit. Touch up the finish (See pages 82 to 83).

Replacing broken corners

You can rebuild a damaged wood corner with wood filler products, and many professionals do it this way. But it's generally better to use real wood, in the form of a wood patch, to replace real wood.

Remove the damaged fibers and material with a saw, then plane the area or sand it flat. Cut a patch slightly larger than the damaged area in all dimensions, using the same species of wood. Orient the patch with the grain to get the strongest glue bond. Then, glue the patch into the cutout damaged area. After the glue has set, trim the patch to follow the contours of the surrounding wood. You'll likely need to touch it up to match the rest of the wood (See pages 82 to 83).

Particleboard and medium-density fiberboard (MDF) are used commonly in furnituremaking these days. Owing to their basic structure, they're more susceptible to crushed corners than natural wood—and less likely to be repaired successfully with the techniques prescribed above.

Crushed or broken corners in particleboard furniture can be rebuilt with polyester-based filler material (such as *Bondo* auto body filler) or similar products made specifically for wood repair. Start by cutting away damaged material and driving in several panhead screws to reinforce the filler. Mix the filler according to the instructions and apply it, using nonstick "dams" to prevent the filler from sagging or dripping. It cures hard (30 minutes to an hour), but from about five to 15 minutes after mixing, it will be a rubbery solid and can be easily carved or roughed out to basic shape with a sharp chisel. After it starts to get hard, it can be easily sanded or filed to final shape. After one hour it's ready for a finish.

HOW TO REBUILD A PARTICLEBOARD CORNER

1 Clean loose chips and shards from the edge of the broken corner, using a utility knife. If the workpiece has a hard surface that has been damaged, it may be necessary to re-cut the corner cleanly (See step 1, previous page). Protect the hard surface with masking tape along the cutting line, and cut with a fine-tooth blade.

2 Drill pilot holes and drive several panhead wood screws into the exposed edge of the damaged area. Be sure to drive the screws straight and deep enough that their heads are well within the lines created by the edges of the workpiece. The screws will provide reinforcement for the filler material in much the same way that rebar reinforces concrete.

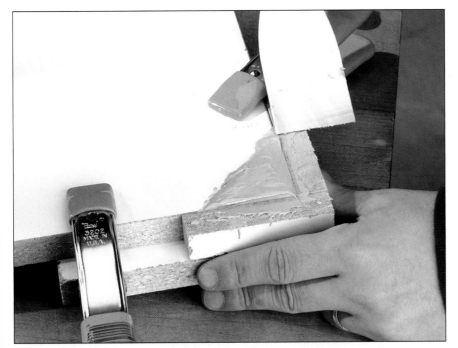

3 Cut small "forms" to attach to the edges and underside of the workpiece, surrounding the damaged corner. Use material with a nonstick surface, such as melamine, to make the forms. Attach the edge forms to the workpiece so their tops are flush with the top surface of the workpiece and they form a clean corner. Attach the bottom form. Prepare a mixture of polyester-based filler material, according to the manufacturer's instructions. Fill the repair area with the filler product. You'll have a couple of minutes of open working time to shape the filler before it becomes too hard to work. Try to get as smooth a surface as possible.

4 Sand and paint the repair. Paint the entire patch, overlapping it slightly into the original section of the panel. Use spray acrylics to match the color. Topcoat with spray-on, nonyellowing acrylic.

Going to the Source of the Problem

A cracked top caused by a basic design flaw won't keep this plant stand down.

There are factors that can cause a piece of furniture to end up as a candidate for repair and refinishing: general wear and tear, abuse, poor quality materials, to name a few. But sometimes furniture fails because of a simple design flaw. When this Mission-style plant stand was built, obvious care was taken to choose nice quality white oak. The mortise-and-tenon joints were carefully made. And even though someone decided to paint it along the way, the original finish was well applied and gave good protection to the wood. But the designer made one critical

The lack of any allowance for wood movement caused the old plant stand to fracture along the glue line.

oversight: he failed to provide expansion relief for the edge-glued tabletop. So, after a few years of expansion and contraction with nowhere to go, the built-up pressure finally

We removed and reglued the split top, then stripped off the paint and old finish materials, using chemical stripper. We also stripped the frame of the plant stand, which was in fine condition and needed no repairs.

After all the parts were stripped, we wiped them down with mineral spirits to neutralize the stripper and clean up any residue it had left behind.

To prevent the top from splitting again, we drilled new holes adjacent to the original screw holes in the glue blocks, creating slots to accommodate the screws used to hold the top in place.

After the new finish was applied to the entire plant stand, we attached the top by running screws up through the slots. We screwed into only the two long edges that are perpendicular to the glue line.

released itself in the weakest spot it could find: along the glue line.

Fortunately, repairing it was not difficult. We simply removed it and reglued it. But before we reattached it, we drilled slotted holes in the glue blocks in the top of the frame. Driven through the slotted holes, the new screws that hold the top in place can shift just enough to allow the top to expand and contract.

~MJ

Skills used in this project:

• *Repairing cracks (pages 56 to 57)*

• *Removing a finish with methylene chloride (pages 106 to 108)*

• *Staining wood (pages 132 to 136)*

• *Applying a finish (pages 128 to 155)*

One of the most common mistakes made by refinishers (beginners and experts alike) is removing an old finish that is better left mostly undisturbed. Often, an unattractive or worn finish can be granted new life simply by touching up a few minor surface problems and giving the surface a thorough cleaning. Not only is repairing a finish a cleaner and faster process than removing and replacing the entire finish, it usually helps preserve the value of antique furnishings.

Repairing a Finish

When many woodworkers see an old dirty finish, their first thought is to remove it. In some cases, this is the best approach. But very often, the finish may simply be in need of some minor repairs or cleaning.

Much of the patina on old wood is on the outer surface of the wood, underneath the finish. The patina is caused by the slow-cooking exposure to sun and air, and has a type of beauty that cannot be replicated with a new finish. The chemicals in most strippers "pull out" some of this patina, which can degrade the desirable characteristics of an old piece. Conservators of antique and historically important furniture rarely remove a finish, only doing so when the finish has degraded to the point that the stability of the piece is jeopardized. Most of the time, the finish is partially removed, which involves the removal of the damaged surface layer only. Almost all techniques involve some type of clean-

ing and removal of accumulations of dirt, oils and old polishes from years of use.

In addition to a good cleaning up or partial removal of the top finish layer, simply fixing a few scratches and dents can dramatically improve the appearance of the finish. The finishing materials on furniture vary in protective ability, durability and appearance. However, they all share one common feature: they react to the forces of light, moisture, air and general wear-and-tear. Finishes may yellow or oxidize, become brittle and crack, or simply become scratched, dented and scraped. While certain finishes will fare better than others, all finishes need some type of routine maintenance and cleaning, and the inevitable dent or scratch needs attention. All of these can be accomplished without stripping the finish.

Sunlight and oxygen combine in a process called

Evaluating a finish: The Scratch Test

Performing this test on a scratched area will help you determine if the scratch penetrates completely through the finish and into the wood, or is confined to the upper finish layers only.

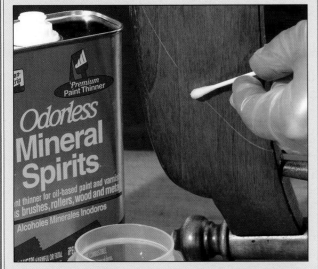

Apply mineral spirits to a scratch with a cotton-tipped applicator. If the scratch disappears, it is confined to the finish layer and the entire scratch can be removed by dissolving the finish around it.

If the scratch lightens but does not disappear, it has cut through both the stain and the finish layer. You'll need to remove the finish over the scratch, re-color the wood and repair the finish layer.

Evaluating a finish: The Solvent Test

Performing this test will help you identify the original finish type that was applied to the piece.

Apply a few drops of denatured alcohol onto the wood finish in an inconspicuous area.

Wait 30 seconds or so, then dab the area where the alcohol was applied with a tissue. If the tissue sticks to the moist area, the finish is shellac. If the tissue does not stick, retest with mineral spirits—a sticky spot will indicate the finish is oil/varnish. If neither solvent becomes sticky, retest with lacquer thinner (stickiness indicates a lacquer finish). If no solvent causes stickiness, the finish is either polyurethane or a modern, commercially applied finish.

photo-oxidation, which causes most of the damage to finishes (as well as to the wood itself). It causes dyes and some pigments to fade, and causes finishes to become brittle and oxidized (marked by cracking and crazing and a dull appearance). Strong sunlight produces heat that can warp wood and cause it to split and crack. Prolonged exposure to high moisture will cause glue joints to fail and finishes to turn white or cloudy. High heat combined with moisture will turn some lacquer finishes dark yellow.

The way to avoid these problems in the first place is simple: keep your furniture out of strong sunlight and avoid storing it in high heat and moisture. Avoid damp areas like basements. If you have large picture windows, consider curtains or window tints to keep colors from fading.

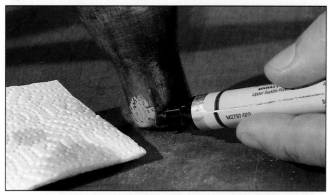

Pens or markers can be used to touch up minor scratches quickly, easily and accurately, without affecting the surrounding areas of the finish.

"Scratch cover" is mineral spirits with a colorant, usually asphaltum, added. You wipe it on and let it sit for a minute or so, then wipe the excess off. You can apply it selectively—just to the damaged area. Normally, you apply the substance to the cloth first and then wipe it into the scratch or apply it directly to the surrounding wood surface.

Repairing scratches

Scratches in wood furniture are repaired in different ways, depending on two variables: the depth of the scratch (whether it goes through stain to bare wood); and the location of the scratch. Deep scratches or scrapes on the surface of wood can always be repaired by stripping, sanding and refinishing, but there are several repair techniques that can mitigate or completely disguise damage with considerably less effort.

The type of finish and the sheen will affect how "invisible" a repaired area is. "Evaporative" finishes like lacquer and shellac are the easiest to repair, because new finish applied to the old will melt into it. "Reactive" finishes like varnish and polyurethane are very difficult to repair. Also, flat and matte (satin) finishes are easier to repair than high-gloss finishes. Finally, a scratch, dent or gouge that's located on the side or near a corner will be easier to repair "invisibly" than a dent in the center of a table.

The first step when evaluating a scratch is to determine whether only the finish layer is scratched, or if the finish, stain and wood surface layers all are damaged (See *The Scratch Test,* previous page). This can be easily determined by wiping the scratch with mineral spirits or naphtha. If the scratch seems to disappear completely after you wipe on the solvent, just the finish is affected. If the scratched area appears lighter, then both the stain and finish are damaged.

The second step is to determine the type of finish you have and how easy it will be to repair (See *The Solvent Test,* previous page). Find an inconspicuous spot, such as under the top or a leg, and dab a couple of drops of denatured alcohol onto the finish surface. Wait 30 seconds or so then rub some tissue into the

HOW TO RUB OUT A FINISH SCRATCH

1 Dry-sand the scratch lightly with 600-grit sandpaper.

2 Rub out the surrounding finish area with 0000 steel wool to blend in the repair area.

3 Use polishing compound and a rag to restore the repaired area to its original sheen, matching the surrounding finish.

HOW TO FILL A DEEP SCRATCH

1 Use dry pigment powder to color a small amount of clear shellac or lacquer to match the stained wood tone. This will take a little trial-and-error. Keep in mind that the color will dry lighter than when it's wet (but the finish will restore some of the darkness). Overfill the scratch slightly.

alcohol spot. If the tissue sticks, then the finish is shellac. If not, repeat the test with lacquer thinner. If the tissue sticks, the finish is lacquer. If neither of these work, the finish is varnish or a catalyzed finish and repairs can still be done, but may not be invisible.

Scratch repair

There are three good ways to fix scratches. Which method you choose depends on the location and depth of the scratch, as well as your skill level:

1. Scratch cover. "Scratch cover" is a commercial mineral spirits product with a colorant, usually asphaltum, added. Like any oil polish, it may also have mineral oil and a fragrance added to disguise the petroleum smell. Unlike traditional oil polishes, the asphaltum does not evaporate. It stays behind to keep the scratch disguised. Scratch cover only hides or partially disguises the scratch and if the scratch is deep, the scratch will be visible from certain viewing angles. Nonetheless, the benefits of using scratch cover are in the application. You wipe it on and let it sit for a minute of so, then wipe the excess off. You can apply it selectively—just to the damaged area—and you can apply it to the cloth and then wipe it in or apply it directly to the wood. Scratch cover is best applied to legs, aprons and other "non-critical" surfaces. At best it should be considered a "quick fix." Do not apply scratch cover if the finish is badly crazed or cracked.

2. Sanding. If the finish is thick enough, or if it's a reactive finish like varnish or polyurethane, your best bet is to sand the scratches out, starting with 600-grit sandpaper. If the 600-grit won't remove the scratch, try switching to 400-grit, but don't use anything coarser. While the traditional method calls for wet-sanding, dry-sanding with very fine sandpaper lets you see what you're doing (wet-sanding gives you a false illusion of finish thickness, increasing the likelihood that you'll accidentally sand through the finish). If the scratches are light, you can work the scratched areas selectively with the 600-grit, but if the scratches are deep, you may want to sand the entire area to avoid hollows created by working one area too aggressively.

3. Apply more finish. If the finish is too thin to sand

2 Rub the repair area with 600-grit sandpaper to knock it down to level with the surrounding finish.

3 Buff the repair area with 0000 steel wool and polishing compound until the new finish material is the same sheen as the surrounding finish surface.

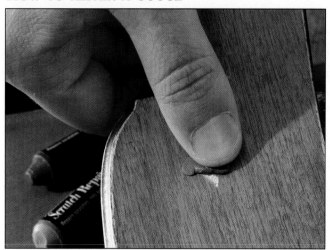

1 Select a finish repair crayon (See previous page) that matches the color of your finish. Slice off a chunk and press it into the gouge.

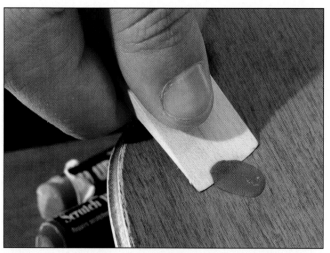

2 Scrape a wedge-shape piece of scrap wood (a wood shim works) across the the top of the wax repair to strike the wax off so it's level with the wood surface.

3 Use the smooth **back** side of a piece of sandpaper to buff the repair and blend it in with the wood.

out the scratch without going through the finish, the best way to repair scratches is to apply more finish product. If the finish is an evaporative finish like lacquer or shellac, scratches will disappear and blend in with the new finish, as long as the scratches are not too deep. For oil finishes that are lightly scratched, apply more oil and wet-sand it in to remove the scratch. If the scratches are deep, it's best if you fill the scratch with finish before applying more finish over the entire surface. This only works for lacquer and shellac finishes (and sometimes for water-based finishes). Fill the scratch with finish by applying some lacquer or shellac with a fine artist's brush. Several applications with overnight drying may be needed. When the scratch has been filled, level-sand the scratch with sandpaper, then apply more finish to the whole area. When the finish is dry, rub it out to the sheen that you want. If the scratch is deep and white, and the finish is varnish or water-based, you'll be better off stripping and refinishing if you want a perfect repair.

Repairing scratches near an edge.

Scrapes or scratches on an edge or corner usually can be repaired easily. When they occur in the center of a top or side they are handled differently. Large scrapes that occur in the center of a side or top are harder to repair. It's best if you strip and refinish the area.

If the finish is the only part that's scraped off, you can apply more finish. If you're not sure whether the finish or part of the wood coloring is gone, wet the damaged area with naphtha. If the "wet" surface blends in with the rest of the finish, then you only have to apply more finish to improve the appearance. Just spray or brush on the finish, let it dry, then smooth it with fine steel wool to blend it in. You can match the original sheen of gloss, satin or dull by rubbing with 0000 steel wool. Or if it's available, spray the appropriate sheen on the scrape. If both color and finish are missing, the naphtha will make the scrape lighter than the rest of the finish when you wet it. In this case, you'll need to replace the original color first, then apply finish. The easiest way to replace color is with a repair pen or marker. Alternatively, you can mix some dry pigment with shellac. Pens are far easier to use and are available in paint and hardware stores. The color selection is limited, but you can combine colors to match most wood tones.

Apply the color to the wood. A good general rule is to leave it lighter than the finished wood surface because most color deepens when the finish is applied over. If the color is too light, you can apply more color. If it's too dark, wipe it immediately with a rag to lighten it. If it's the wrong color, apply another color over it. A naphtha-moistened rag will remove most color completely if it's way off. When the color is dry, seal it in with finish of the appropriate sheen or rub down the gloss with 0000 steel wool.

1 Choose a burn-in stick (also called a "shellac stick") that closely matches the color of your wood finish. Melt a small chunk of the material onto the end of an electric burn-in knife (if you work quickly, you can try heating the blade of a palette knife with a candle flame).

2 Press the molten material into the gouge or dent with the tip of the knife.

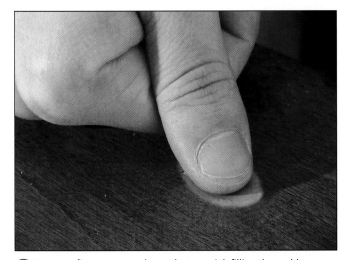

3 Use your finger to smooth out the material, filling the problem area. Work quickly so the material does not harden before you're finished shaping it.

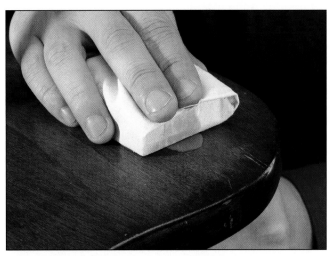

4 Wrap a wood block with muslin (or any other lightweight, semi-coarse cloth), dab some alcohol onto the cloth and buff the repair until it is smooth with the surrounding surface.

Gouges, dents, chips & burns

Gouges, dents and other problems are repaired by filling the depression with a colored substance to imitate the color of the surrounding wood. In some cases the damage can be repaired without stripping or removing the finish and in these cases two products are used, colored wax and stick shellac (also known as burn-in sticks). Of the two, colored wax is the easiest, but stick shellac is harder, so it's better for areas that will get more wear and tear.

To use wax on a small dent or gouge, rub the wax crayon along the gouge. Then rub the excess off with a soft cloth wrapped around a small block of wood. If you rub it too much you'll remove the wax, so rub just until it's level.

To fill larger gouges with wax, rub the area with the crayon or cut off a small piece and jam it in the depression. Then, using a "chisel" made from a small piece of wood, pare the excess wax off until it's level with the surface. Then, use the smooth back of a piece of sandpaper to rub the wax level with the surface.

Burn-in sticks are a bit harder to use and you can damage the surface around the gouge or dent if you're not careful. The general procedure is to melt or "burn-in" a chunk of the stick with a hot knife. You can purchase electric burn-in knives inexpensively at most woodworking supply stores. Or, you may be able to get by with an artist's palette knife heated over a candle flame. Once the material has melted, quickly press

1 Puncture the finish in the dented area with a stainless steel pin to allow the steam to work its way underneath the finish surface.

2 Lightly dampen a clean rag and lay it over the dent. Apply the tip of a household iron, set on high, to the rag, directly above the dent.

3 Remove the rag and iron. If the dent has shrunk, but not fully disappeared, repeat until it's gone.

down with your finger to push the resin into the depression. If the burn-in material is shellac-based, the repair is best leveled by wrapping a piece of muslin around a small piece of wood, then wetting it slightly with alcohol and rubbing the repair. If the burn-in material is based on another type of resin, or the original finish is not shellac, level the repair by sanding very carefully with fine sandpaper lubricated with mineral spirits. When the burn-in is leveled, you can adjust the color by using touch-up pigments mixed with shellac or lacquer, then painting in any missing grain lines

to imitate the wood grain. Topcoat the repair with a finishing product.

Cigarette burns are repaired by removing the charred wood with a gouge or chisel, then filling the area. It's best to use stick shellac as a filler because you generally have to remove a fair amount of wood, and stick shellac is harder and more durable than wax. Putty or wood dough can be used, but several applications may need to be applied because it shrinks as it dries. If you use wood filler, choose a latex or water-based product and apply it so the surface domes

Abrading a finish

Cleaning a finish removes the surface dirt from the finish, but it still may be hazy or whitish. Part of this problem may be from small crazing or cracks in the finish that reflect light, making the surface appear dull. If this is the case and the cracks do not go all the way through to the wood, abrading part of the finish will remove most of the cracks. Use *stearated sandpaper* (sandpaper mixed with zinc stearate to minimize clogging) to abrade away a portion of the finish. Start with 240-grit and proceed to 320-grit and finally 400-grit. Back the paper with your hand only (no sanding blocks) to avoid sanding though high spots and to help you go easy around the edges. Wear a dust mask, since the dust is irritating. Sand in straight lines, with the finish, and wipe the residue off frequently with a rag dampened in naphtha or mineral spirits. You can stop sanding when the grain of the wood is visible or when the cracks have disappeared. Patience is required because a heavy hand will cut through the finish and you'll have no choice but to strip at that point. Wipe the piece with naphtha or mineral spirits when you're finished and let it dry overnight.

slightly, allowing for some shrinkage. When it's dry, you can easily "sand" it by rubbing it with a damp cloth wrapped around a wood block. When dry, touch it up with color and grain it.

Rings and water spots. Next to scratches, rings and water spots are the most common types of damage finishes undergo. They may be easily removed, depending upon the nature of the damage to the wood or the finish, and how the damage occurred. The color of the ring dictates what to do.

Black rings. If the color is black or gray, the damage is from water that has permeated the finish and discolored the wood below. The most common form of this damage is from pots or vases that allow water to wick under the base of the pot. The water is never seen until the pot or vase is removed, and by then it's too late. To repair this damage, strip the finish, sand the wood and bleach it with oxalic acid (See pages 123 to 125).

White rings. If the ring is white, the damage is from water or heat and is generally located in the finish layer only. The damage may be on top of the finish or at the bottom, where the finish meets the wood. Top damage is easily repaired. If the damage is at the bottom layer of the finish, however, it's probably caused by heat and is rarely repairable. There's no easy way to tell where the damage is located, other than to try a sequence of steps and see if any are effective.

Most superficial damage can be rubbed out with steel wool and either oil, rubbing compound or fine sandpaper. The whiteness disappears fairly quickly and, once removed, the finish can be rubbed out to the original sheen. If the finish is lacquer or shellac, a light padding with a rag moistened with alcohol will remove the white spot. Wipe the rag in a back-and-forth motion to remove the white spot. If neither of these work, strip the finish (See pages 100 to 111) or learn to live with the problem.

HOW TO REMOVE WHITE RINGS FROM A FINISH

Option 1

OPTION ONE: Many times, a white ring in a finish can be removed simply by buffing the surface lightly with polishing compound, working in a circular motion. Try this method first.

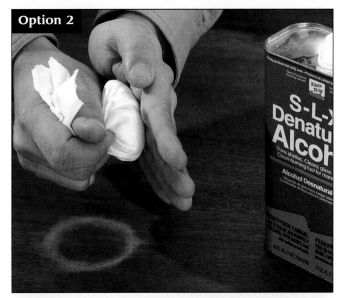

Option 2

OPTION TWO:
1 Wad several clean rags together into a ball and dampen them with denatured alcohol.

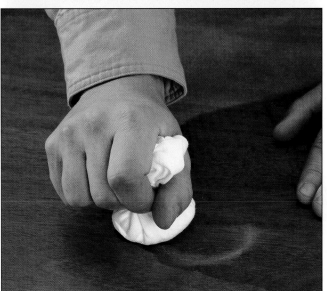

2 Work the alcohol-soaked wad of rags back and forth over the white ring in a pendulum motion until the ring disappears.

Restoring finishes

The goal in restoring an old finish is not to make it look brand new. At best, this treatment should restore as much of the original condition as possible and prevent further deterioration. While restoring a finish is by no means a "quick fix" type of repair, on most pieces it should be less time-consuming and expensive than a complete stripping and refinishing. In addition, you do not run the risk of ruining the value of an old piece of furniture by removing a piece of its history. The following are the steps in saving an old finish: sealing damage, cleaning, abrading the old finish (if necessary) and finally waxing.

NOTE: Although it's a good idea to preserve the original wood finish whenever possible, finishes that have degraded to the point where the wood is in jeopardy should be removed and replaced. These situations include severe water or heat damage, large losses of the finish with exposed wood, and severe discoloration. Severe water or heat damage appear as large white areas where the finish is peeling or flaking off. Large exposed areas of wood are very difficult to blend in even if you have advanced refinishing skills, so removal of the entire finish is called for. Another finish that can-

not be saved is a finish that is sticky. Sticky finishes are those that have become chemically altered to the point where they will never fully harden. Yet another problem finish is one in which the finish has been mixed with pigment and applied thickly. Old varnishes and shellacs applied in this manner may develop large cracks or "islands" which show the bare wood below. This finish should be removed in most cases. Exceptions are crazed or cracked finishes where the cracks do not go all the way through to the wood below.

Seal damaged areas. Damaged areas that should be sealed before any finish restoration work is done include dents, scratches and small areas of finish that have been worn away. The cleaning process involves water and solvents that could possibly affect bare wood, so the wood should be protected. For sealing, use a two-pound cut of light-colored shellac (See pages 135 and 143). Using an artist's brush, apply several light coats of shellac to the damaged area and then let the shellac dry overnight. Do not try to match the color to the surrounding finish at this point. The cleaning will lighten up the color so blending in at this point will result in an eventual mismatch.

removes both water-soluble and oil-soluble dirt and grime. The first cleaning step is to use mineral spirits or naphtha to remove oil-soluble grime. *NOTE: Test a small amount of the cleaner on an inconspicuous area first—it's rare that mineral spirits or naphtha will harm a finish, but it's*

Before

After

A thorough cleaning can have an amazing impact on the overall appearance of an old piece of furniture. Simply wiping the dirty antique chest shown here with mineral spirits then soapy water greatly brightened the appearance.

Cleaning a finish

Before properly cleaning a piece of wood furniture, you should know what material was used for the finish so the appropriate cleaners can be used (See *Evaluating the Finish: The Solvent Test,* page 73). Knowing which finish you have minimizes possible damage from cleaning solvents.

Furniture cleaning is a two-step process that

worth a check. If your test spot turns white, and you want to save the finish, proceed to the abrading and/or waxing step below. If the test spot doesn't change color, dampen a clean cloth with the naphtha and rub a small surface at a time. Do not saturate the surface. Switch to clean cloths frequently.

The second cleaning step involves using a detergent (liquid dishwashing detergent is effective and readily available) mixed with distilled water.

How to Clean a Wood Finish

1 Seal any damaged areas, like nicks or dents, with shellac applied with a small artist's brush.

2 Fill a shallow pan with mineral spirits and, wearing rubber gloves, dip a clean, tightly woven and lint-free rag into the mineral spirits. Press the rag against the side of the container to force excess liquid out. Wash all surfaces with mineral spirits, moving the rag in a circular pattern to remove the maximum amount of oil-soluble grime. Inspect the rag often, changing to a fresh rag when it becomes soiled.

3 Once the mineral spirits have evaporated, mix a pint of warm water with a couple of teaspoons of mild dishwashing detergent (preferably, one that contains a grease-cutting agent). Use more clean rags to wash the surface again with the new solution, removing mineral spirits residue and other water-soluble agents.

4 Dry the wood surfaces completely with a soft, lint-free towel as soon as you finish washing each part of the furniture piece. Apply two or three coats of paste wax to protect the finish.

Blending in a finish repair

Whenever you splice in a new piece of wood or replace veneer, you'll have to blend the new wood finish in with the old. When done with the right materials and a few pointers in the right direction, even beginners can achieve decent results. Essentially, you have to remember two things: One, wood is not a solid, opaque color; it's built up of layers of translucent colors, so it's best if you proceed in light applications of color, building it slowly. Two, sometimes the color of wood shifts from light to dark when you view it from different angles, so look at the area you're touching up from different angles as you work on it.

The first step is to make sure the new wood is leveled to the old part by sanding it with sandpaper, wrapped around a hard block of wood. Start with 120-grit, then switch to 150- and finally go up to 220-grit. When done, remove the dust with a rag. To visualize what color you need to color the new wood, dampen the repair area with mineral spirits. The wet wood will deepen a bit and allow you to see what the color would be with a finish applied. Then, mix a water-soluble dye stain to the color you need, using several different colors, if necessary. Wipe some dye on the wood. A water-soluble dye will color only new, bare wood, without affecting surrounding finished wood. The color of the wet dye will be the same as the final color after the finish is applied. You can change the color by adding a different dye color. Let the dye dry.

Spray or wipe a seal coat of shellac over the dye. Then, using a fine-pointed artist's brush and dry pigments mixed with shellac or lacquer, paint in the fine background lines of wood grain. Seal with more finish (an aerosol spray is preferred so as not to disturb the grain lines you painted). Adjust the color of the dye or blend in the area between the new and old wood, if visible, with pigment mixed with shellac or lacquer. When you're happy with the result, apply several coats of finish in the sheen you want. Or, apply gloss finish and rub it with 0000 steel wool to blend it in to match the original sheen.

1 Sand as needed to level any new wood repair areas with the surrounding wood surface. Apply a dab of mineral spirits to the new wood patch or raw wood to approximate the color the unstained wood would be with a clear topcoat applied. If the tones match, skip to Step 3.

4 Use pigments to tint some shellac to match any dark grain lines in the original wood that are interrupted by the repair wood. Extend the existing grain lines into the repair area, using a fine artist's brush.

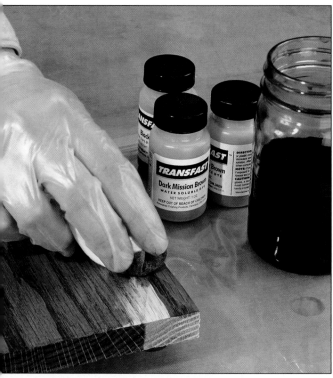

2 Blend water-soluble dyes in a water solution to attempt to match the tone and color of the original wood finish. Apply dye to match the background color. When you achieve a good match, apply the dye to the repair area.

3 Seal the colored wood surface with thinned, clear shellac (dewaxed) to prevent additional colorants from soaking into the wood fibers.

5 Spray a few light coats of protective finish onto the repair area (brushing or wiping on a topcoat may smear or erase the dark grain lines you've painted).

6 Once the new finish has dried, buff or rub out the surface to match the surrounding wood, using 0000 steel wool or a very fine synthetic steel wool pad.

AFTER

BEFORE

Resolving an Identity Crisis

A humble English chest, cut apart long ago and forced into service as an awkward basin stand, goes back to its roots.

Once upon a time in a country called England there was a simple but elegant wooden chest. For many years it served its owners well, providing safe haven for blankets, linens and treasured pieces of finery. Then one day the owners of the chest decided that they no longer needed it. Instead, they wanted to have a new piece of furniture: a standing cabinet for the family wash basin, perhaps even with a shelf or two. So they got busy. They turned the chest on end and replaced the

lid with a cabinet door. They added shelves inside the main cavity—now vertical. They fashioned four crude feet and attached them to the end of the chest. Finally, they found an old curio shelf, cut it down in width and nailed it to the other end of the chest—now the top. When the transformation was complete, they added a coat of bright paint to try and blend the many parts that had been brought together. It was an ugly contraption, to be sure, but it fulfilled its purpose and that's what mattered the most.

The old pine chest you see in the "Before" photo was purchased at an auction in England. It was originally built some time in the 19th century. The transformation described above probably occurred near the turn of the 20th century, as best we can tell. When we saw the thing for

(RIGHT) The first step in restoring this old chest was to get rid of the many new parts that had been added to convert the chest to a basin stand. These included the feet, the upper shelving and the cabinet door. The parts came off easily, as the wood was deteriorated and softened in many areas. But the softness also demanded that we use some extra care to avoid causing more damage.

the first time, we really didn't know how to react: It was a little like watching the kids dress the family dog up in play clothes—you don't know whether to laugh at the old mutt or feel sorry for it. Ultimately, we felt sorry for the chest and, after some careful investigation and a bit of guesswork, we decided to help it find its way back to becoming a chest again.

Once we'd removed the upper shelf and the feet that had been added, we stripped off the many coats of paint and discovered that the front of the chest was decorated with carvings that probably are not original. Still, it did give the chest some interest, so we cleaned them up a bit. Next, we pried off the mitered face frame that was added for the cabinet door, which replaced the original chest lid. We reglued the hand-cut dovetails at the corners—the wood had deteriorated in several spots, weakening the joints. In fact, there was quite a bit of wood loss, especially near the bottom of the chest. To compensate for the wood loss, we made the difficult decision to add some beefy base trim. From a strict restorationist standpoint, adding new parts is a bit of a last resort, but our concern was mainly to preserve the structural integrity of the piece. And because we needed to make a brand new lid for the chest, the historical restoration approach was already ceded. Because of this, we knew we weren't dealing with an especially valuable or important piece, but the end result was successful for a couple of reasons. Restored to its original form, the chest has a certain primitive charm, strong visual interest and, perhaps best of all, a good story behind it.

~MJ

(ABOVE) The original chest lid had been removed and replaced with a face frame and a cabinet door. Like the other "new" parts, the mitered face frame came off with very little resistance. One of the saving graces of questionable repair/restoration work is that the workmanship tends to be sloppy and more easy to reverse than careful, professional

(LEFT) After stripping the many layers of old paint, we learned two new things about the chest: someone (probably not the original builder) had carved a pair of potted tulips into the front panel, and the wood around the joints was in worse condition than we thought. Because the tulip carvings are sawed off at the top, it's likely that the entire chest was cut down a bit, perhaps as part of its conversion into a basin stand. Enough wood was gone that it was necessary to reglue and clamp the hand-cut dovetail joints at the chest corners. Because we were dealing with a very old piece, we used yellow PVA glue (still a bit of a compromise), but on a newer piece with this much damage we would have opted for polyurethane glue for its gap-filling properties.

The Value Question

The recent revival of interest in antiques, particularly owing to television shows and the Internet, has created the perception that every old piece of furniture is a treasure piece in disguise, just waiting to make its owner rich. Of course, this is as far from true today as it ever was. The fact is, the vast majority of old furniture pieces have only very modest monetary value, whether restored or not. The best reason to buy old furniture, or to choose to invest a lot of time or money in a piece, is still this: "Because you like it."

(ABOVE) We were concerned about the poor condition of the chest panels and corners, especially near the bottom. Even after regluing, the joints seemed a bit fragile. So we decided to add some thick pine base trim to reinforce the chest, at the same time creating "feet" by overhanging the panels slightly. The "feet" allow the chest to sit cleanly on the floor, without rocking, and also protect the bottom panel from ground contact. We made the mitered trim from plain pine, cutting chamfers at the top.

(RIGHT) To build a new lid for the chest, we salvaged some pine from an old tabletop. After planing and jointing it, we edge-glued the boards to form a rough panel for the top. Once the glue had set, we trimmed it down to finished size on the table saw. To better blend in with the rest of the chest, we did a little bit of distressing to the surface, creating a handful of nicks and dents to give the lid some "age." It's important not to go overboard when distressing wood, however, so we used a fairly light touch.

Skills used in this project:

• *Regluing dovetail joints (page 51)*

• *Making replacement parts (pages 56 to 59)*

• *Removing a finish (pages 100 to 111)*

• *Sanding (pages 118 to 121)*

• *Applying a finish (pages 128 to 155)*

(ABOVE) We stained the chest box first, after light hand-sanding, to see what the stain would do to the color. Then we stained the new lid. We used a slightly darker stain on the lid because the newer pine wasn't as thirsty and therefore didn't absorb as much stain. The match ended up being pretty close. We attached the new lid with butt hinges (after doing some reinforcement to the wood in the hinge areas), then applied two coats of paste wax for a natural-looking finish.

Simply cleaning and polishing old, dingy hardware can make a dramatic improvement in the appearance of a worn-out looking piece of furniture. When done in concert with a full restoration, refurbishing hardware gives your project a fresh finishing touch.

Refurbishing Hardware

Hardware is subjected to constant stress and a considerable amount of hand contact. As a result, the pulls, knobs, hinges, latches and other hardware items on a piece of furniture require both regular maintenance and occasional repair. And because the parts are generally metal, not wood, the techniques and products use to spruce up or completely refurbish hardware are quite different than those used for wood repairs.

The most common hardware problem is stripping out of the screws that attach the hardware to the wood. Hinges and pulls are famous for this. There are a number of remedies you can use to fix stripped screws, from quick treatments that are destined to result in a recurrence of the problem, to fairly complicated wood replacement "therapy." A reasonably durable (and easy) repair option is shown on the next page. A similar technique is also explained on pages

Hardware plates can contort from pressure or during removal. Because they're relatively soft metal, they can be straightened out easily simply by hammering them flat on a sturdy worksurface, like the bench vise seen here.

50 to 51). Although it directly affects the metal hardware and its performance, repairing a stripped screw or screws is a wood repair job, so you should keep the primary directive in mind: Always replace wood with wood.

In addition to weakening of its connection to the wood, metal hardware rusts, breaks, contorts, pits, gums up, tarnishes and undergoes a host of other problems. In many cases, the best solution is to replace the hardware with new parts. Particularly with mass-produced furniture, the hardware styles have changed very little over the years, making locating a matching replacement part a reasonable option. If you can't find the correct part at your local hardware store, check woodworking and furniture restoration supply catalogs. There are even catalog suppliers that specialize in restoration hardware. You may be amazed at the selection.

Replacing a single piece of hardware has its drawbacks, though. For one, it will be very obvious. There are techniques you can use to artificially age new metal (See pages 90 to 91), which can help. Or, if the hardware is cheap and more than one piece are in questionable condition, consider replacing all the similar hardware on the piece—this is done frequently with pulls and knobs.

Yet another option is to try to repair damaged hardware. It's possible to fix most pieces made of non-ferrous metals (including brass or copper) by resoldering it. This is done with silver solder and a propane torch, and using flux to allow the solder to flow smoothly. In the case of ferrous parts (iron and steel), soldering is not an option, so you'll either need to replace the part or find someone in your area to recast it. Or, you can try recasting a replacement yourself (See pages 96 to 97).

Because they are aesthetic and not structural, many common hardware problems are remedied with surface treatments, not metal repairs. In most cases, you'll want to remove the hardware first so you can treat it thoroughly. Removing rust, lubricating moving parts, cleaning up tarnishing, polishing and chemical alteration of the patina are a few of the metal treatment techniques you'll find helpful.

HOW TO REPAIR A STRIPPED SCREW HOLE

1 Door hinges, even cabinet door hinges, receive major stress and shear pressure that often lead to screws stripping out of the wood. Once the wood is stripped, redriving the screw will not help. To properly address the problem, start by removing the hardware (always remove the lower hinges first).

2 Use a ⅜-in. Forstner or brad-point bit to drill out the damaged wood in the repair area. Try to keep the hole centered and straight. Then, apply glue to a hardwood screw plug (most are ⅜-in. dia.) and insert it into the hole. Set it with a few gentle taps from a mallet until it's flush.

3 Once the glue has dried, drill a new pilot hole into the plug and reattach the hinge. For best results, use a self-centering Vix bit to drill the pilot hole (you'll need to temporarily attach the hinge plate in correct position before drilling—tape works well).

AFTER

Metal hardware, both brand new and recently stripped, can be finished with any number of products and processes to alter its appearance. The drawer pull shown on these pages was one of six that were attached to the drawers on an antique walnut dresser (See cover photo and page 6). The pulls had been painted with cheap gold-tone spray paint (See photo, below). We stripped them clean, then tested several different patination techniques to see which one would look best on the refinished project. Here are the results.

BEFORE

(Above) Dark pigment stain is applied to the pull. The stain settles into the low areas, enhancing the appearance of depth and dimension. Excess stain is dabbed from the nonrecessed areas with a paper towel before it dries. Prior to applying the stain, the pull was stripped with lacquer thinner and sealed with shellac. More shellac is applied after the stain.

Patination

If you replace a piece of old hardware (or even strip and clean old hardware on an old piece of furniture), you'll generally want to match the original patina or color as closely as possible. *Patination* is the term used for the process of making new or stripped metal look old or worn. There are two basic options for patination: with chemicals (and chemical reactions) or with application of coloring agents.

With either method, you must start with clean, unfinished metal. Almost all new hardware has some kind of protective finish applied that needs to be removed for coloring agents to stick or for chemical reactions to occur uniformly and predictably. To remove old finishes, soak the hardware in stripper overnight and then brush it with a soft-bristle brush or 00 steel wool. Then rinse it in lacquer thinner (See page 92).

Chemical patination. The most common chemical patination process is to blacken or darken brass and copper. While there are a few household cleaning chemicals that can affect the appearance and color of the metal, the best products to use are commercially produced patination compounds. Most of

these are simply applied with a brush. Then, when the metal turns the desired color, the action is stopped by rinsing with water. Highlights can be created, if desired, with steel wool (See page 93).

Coloring. Pigment stains can be used to impart color to metal. This is particularly effective when you want to get dark color into crevices or low areas, which adds dimension to the hardware. After stripping and rinsing in lacquer thinner (See page 92), rub the metal with 00 steel wool. Apply a dark brown pigment stain and wipe the excess off, leaving the dark stain just in the low spots. Let it dry and then apply a clear lacquer (See page 94).

Brass and other metals will oxidize if not protected with a clear finish. If you don't want to finish the metal, that's fine, but you'll have to use a brass polish on it frequently to renew it. If you want to avoid polishing, apply a clear brass lacquer or use shellac. Shellac is easier to find and was used for centuries as a metal coating. Apply it any way you wish, and pick a color (either clear or orange) that suits your taste. On old hardware, orange shellac is a good way to give the hardware a slight golden color (See page 95).

ADDITIONAL HARDWARE PATINATION OPTIONS

Cleaning only. Simply cleaning the hardware with lacquer thinner and a small brush can yield great results in some cases. This pull was not such a case. After cleaning, seal with shellac or spray lacquer.

Polishing with steel wool. After cleaning with lacquer thinner, the pull is buffed with 00 steel wool to brighten the finish or, in this case, remove the tarnish and a few specs of gold paint that the lacquer thinner failed to dissolve. Seal with spray lacquer or shellac.

Metal polish imparts an added layer of luster to the hardware, bringing out the highlights and increasing depth. The pull above received three applications of polish (See page 92). Be sure to read and follow the polish manufacturer's directions. Seal with spray lacquer or shellac.

A chemical blackening agent reacts with the metal to darken it, giving the appearance of age. Clean the hardware, bathe it in the chemical (See page 93), then buff with steel wool and apply a protective coat of spray lacquer or shellac.

Fuming is a darkening technique traditionally used on oak or cherry, but it will also darken brass or copper. The part is suspended over liquid ammonia in an enclosed container until it darkens, then is rinsed with distilled water to halt the darkening process. Finish with shellac or spray lacquer (See page 95).

Verdigris is the familiar green color of oxidized copper or brass. It will occur naturally over time if the metal is not protected with lacquer or shellac. Or, it can be replicated with a number of commercial finishing products that are designed to create a green patina (See page 93).

HOW TO CLEAN METAL HARDWARE

1 Lacquer thinner is a good, all-purpose hardware cleaning agent. It will cut through most of the oil and grime that accumulate on hardware. (If the hardware is painted, you'll need to use the stripping agent best suited for the type of paint before cleaning in lacquer thinner.) Submerge the hardware in thinner for an hour or two. Then, wearing protective gloves, scrub it with a small, metal-bristled scrub brush. On delicate hardware, use a brush with stiff nylon bristles.

2 (OPTION) Because shiny-like-new hardware will look out of place on an older piece of furniture, you may want to knock down the gloss a bit by buffing with 0000 steel wool after cleaning is done.

3 (OPTION) On the other hand, a bright, shiny finish may be precisely what you're looking for. In that case, polish the hardware with metal polish after cleaning it. Follow the polish manufacturer's directions. To minimize the need for regular polishing in the future, coat the hardware with spray-lacquer or shellac after polishing (See page 95).

1 Clean the hardware thoroughly with lacquer thinner (previous page), then brush the chemical patination solution onto all hardware surfaces. In the photo at right, a commercial blackening agent made for artificially aging metal is being applied. You can find these products in many woodworking supply stores, or in furniture restoration catalogs. Be sure to follow all the manufacturer's usage directions and safety precautions—some of these chemicals are caustic. Allow the chemical to work until the desired tone is achieved, then rinse with distilled water to neutralize the chemical reaction.

1 (OPTION): Another option to the blackening agent shown above is a chemical "greening" formula. When dipped in greening (sometimes called "verdigris") solution, then removed and exposed to the air, copper and brass will turn green. This creates a similar color to the naturally occurring greenish cast created as these metals oxidize over time.

2 After the chemical patination has had the desired effect, and the chemical has been neutralized, buff with 0000 steel wool to knock back the color change in higher areas, as would ordinarily happen if the color change was caused by normal aging and oxidation. Coat with shellac or spray lacquer to preserve the finish.

APPLYING A COLORING AGENT TO HARDWARE

1 Pigment-based wood stains can be used to alter the color tone of metal hardware and to give it greater depth (See examples on pages 90 to 91). Before applying the pigment stain, seal the cleaned hardware with shellac. This will prevent the stain from bonding in an all-over fashion to the hardware.

2 Brush or dab the pigment stain onto the hardware after the shellac has dried. The slick surface of the shellac will cause the stain to pool slightly in the recessed areas of the hardware, yielding a look that is more natural than uniform coloration. Dab away any excess on the "highlight" areas. If you're not happy with the appearance, wipe off all the stain and try again until you get just the look you want. Then, coat the entire piece with more shellac.

FUMING METAL HARDWARE

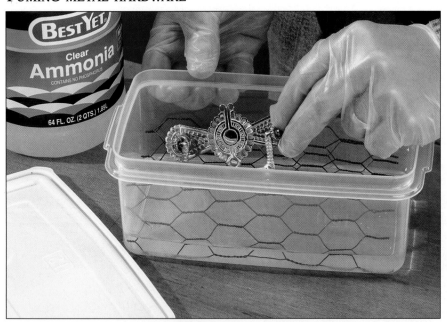

1 Professionals generally fume hardware and wood with highly concentrated ammonia formulations not sold in the general marketplace, but you can get pleasing results with metal hardware using ordinary household ammonia (See photo, page 91, lower left). Because you don't want the piece to come in direct contact with the liquid ammonia, lay some folded chicken wire in the bottom of a plastic container with a lid to bolster the hardware. Pour an inch or so of ammonia into the container, then place the hardware on top of the bolster. Close the lid tightly and let the fumes work on the metal for an hour or two (make sure you clean the metal thoroughly first). Check the results, and fume longer if needed.

2 Once the metal has darkened to the tone you want, dip it in distilled water to neutralize the chemical reaction occurring (don't use harsher neutralizing agents, like vinegar, as they can reverse the fuming process). When dry, buff with 0000 steel wool then coat the metal with spray lacquer or shellac. Dispose of the ammonia properly.

SHELLAC

SPRAY LACQUER

Like wood, metal is vulnerable to moisture and oxidation that can alter its appearance. In some cases, this can yield very beautiful, natural patinas. But if you've put a lot of effort into cleaning or patinating a piece of hardware, protect your investment with a topcoat of clear finish. A thin coat or two of shellac (left) can be applied with a brush for a top-

coat that will bond well without discoloring the metal or affecting the finish gloss. Or, you can spray the hardware with spray lacquer (right). Spray lacquer (the product shown above is specially formulated for application on brass) is quick and easy to apply, as long as you don't lay it on too thickly.

Sagging doors may not be a hinge problem

Sagging cabinet doors can be the result of a hinge that's bent, a hinge pin that's worn, or hinge screws that are stripped. But if the doors are sticking or aren't level at the top, the first thing to do is to try and level the problem out. Check the piece for level first, as a non-level floor will cause sticking doors, and make adjustments at one of the four corners with levelers (if the piece has them) or shims. This will twist the cabinet back into square and the doors will operate fine. If this doesn't work, check for bent hinges. Sight up the gap between the door and

Try shimming a piece of furniture to level it if the doors are sagging or sticking. If this doesn't help, then focus your attention on the hinges.

the cabinet (on the hinge side). If the gap is larger at one of the hinge points, that hinge is probably bent, so remove it and straighten it out with a small hammer with the hinge plate backed up on an anvil, a metal bench vise or a concrete floor. If all else fails, you have no other choice than to plane the doors. If they're sticking at one point, like the top, plane off a small amount in that area only. If they're sticking across the entire length of the door, plane the whole door.

Metal Casters

One of the most common problems with metal casters (rollers) occurs when the wooden roller wears or breaks. Fixing this is a fairly easy repair. On most casters, the pin the roller rides on has a round end and a peened end. The peened end is the flat end that's only slightly mushroomed. File this end to remove the mushroomed material and drive it through with a nailset. Make sure you support the caster end by wedging a piece of wood through the two forks that hold the pin.

Make a new roller from a maple dowel and sand the sharp edges a bit. Drill a hole through the new roller, and insert it between the caster forks. Insert the pin. With the rounded head of the pin resting on an anvil or a metal bench vise, peen the end of the pin by tapping it gently with a hammer (that's what a ball peen hammer is really for).

Casting ornamental hardware

Many ornamental flat brass pieces can be replicated using the simple casting technique shown here. Special casting compound is poured over the hardware to create a mold, then the mold is used to cast a new piece. There are several products that can be used to make the mold and still more used to make the casting. Shown below are a two-part mold-casting compound that's blended and poured in liquid form, and a two-part, polymerized casting compound used to make the actual piece. In addition, to give the resinous replacement part a natural metallic look, the mold is treated with bronzing powder prior to the casting.

For more information on other casting products, see pages 66 to 67 and the manufacturer's reference on page 160.

1 Construct a shallow reservoir for the liquid casting material. We used small strips of melamine-coated particleboard, hot-glued to a flat melamine base. Another option is to build up a round dam of modeling clay on a nonstick surface.

2 Set the hardware piece being replicated into the reservoir, with the "good" face facing up. Prepare the mold-making compound as directed by the manufacturer.

3 Pour the mold-casting compound over the hardware and into the reservoir. Pour in enough so the hardware is covered by at least ¼ in. or so. Follow the manufacturer's directions concerning set-up time.

4 After the mold-casting compound has set, remove the mold and detach it from the hardware. Inspect it closely to make sure it came out well. For a convincing imitation of genuine brass, we dusted the mold with bronzing powder before casting the new piece. See manufacturer's reference, page 160.

5 Pour the casting material into the form. Two-part materials, like the polymerized material shown here, usually are mixed together in a clean vessel before being poured into the mold. Let the material set up as directed.

6 Remove the new decorative hardware from the mold. Use a sharp knife to clean up any rough edges. If you did not use bronzing powder to create a metallic finish, paint the new piece to match. Reuse the mold to cast as many parts as you need.

Chestnut (601)

Aged Oak (602)

Antique Maple (603)

Honey Maple (604)

Mahogany

Walnut

Cherrywood

Brazilian Rosewood

Refinishing & Finishing

Where furniture repair relies mostly on basic woodworking skills, refinishing and finishing furniture is essentially a matter of patience, care and technique. As you gain experience in removing old finishes and applying new ones, you'll pick up a few tricks and tips that make the job easier or neater. But in the final analysis, successful work with finishes is all about taking the time to do it right.

In this section you'll find information identifying the principal products to choose from for finish removal, surface preparation and application of new finishes. You'll also find helpful, step-by-step demonstrations showing you exactly how these products are used.

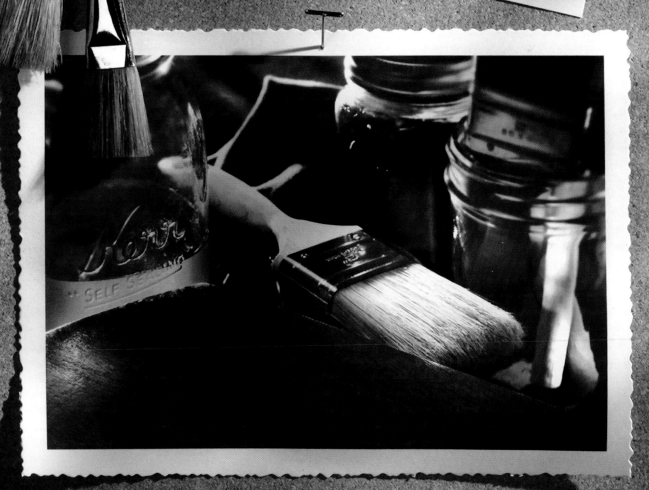

Removing a Finish

Finishes don't last forever. In spite of advances in the durability and quality of finishing materials in the last century, they still are affected by heat, water and sunlight, as well as everyday handling and general wear and tear. When a finish can no longer provide protective qualities, or large areas are missing or sticky, it's time to remove it. Removing a finish may also be done for an appearance change, such as changing the color or making a finish more durable. If the finish is in good shape, and is just dirty or dull looking, we'll look at ways you can revive the finish without stripping.

There's only one word of caution here. It's a fairly well known fact that if you have a valuable piece of furniture, refinishing will affect value. There's no way to tell this unless you consult a professional, and that may be the best option before proceeding with a very old piece with its original finish. On the other hand, if it's a piece that isn't destined for the museum or

antique showroom, there's plenty of satisfaction in restoring a rough piece of furniture back to its former glory, and it's doubtful its value will be affected.

It's at this point we need to discuss two different approaches. One approach is to return the piece to the appearance it had when it was new. This is generally called complete *restoration* and it involves removing the finish, sanding the wood level and filling any dents, gouges and other mishaps, along with restaining, polishing hardware, and replacing worn mirror and glass. The other approach is not as aggressive and leaves dents and general wear-and-tear, as well as the patina, intact. The finish may simply be cleaned or, if necessary, removed, but the wood is not sanded. Hardware is cleaned, but not polished and glass and mirror is left alone. This approach goes by several names, but calling it *limited restoration* sums it up as well as any of them. As the owner of your piece of furniture, you're certainly free to do whatever you want to it, but limited

The Professional Option

Completing every aspect of a furniture restoration project yourself is a satisfying experience, but in some cases you may prefer to hire out some or all of the project. Professional furniture restoration shops, like the one shown here, have the space, equipment and expertise to take on any part of the job. Of all the tasks that make up a full-scale furniture restoration project, stripping off the old finish is the one most people are happiest to have done for them.

Professional refinishers use a variety of methods and products to strip a finish. Many operate so-called "dipping tanks," which are large tubs usually filled with a lye-based stripping agent. The item to be stripped is submerged in the solution to loosen the old finish. While dipping tanks are fine for woodwork (especially if it's going to be painted), they can cause problems in furniture by dissolving glue joins or darkening the wood. But most refinishing shops also offer hand-stripping services, which is done using the same basic techniques and products any do-it-yourselfer would use. Furniture repair, veneer repair and custom finishing services also are offered by most professional shops—along with good advice to help you make decisions about your piece of furniture.

Randy Wackerfuss of Old Science Renovation In Minnesota scrubs down a Windsor-style chair with chemical stripper.

restoration is recommended if you're concerned with keeping patina and an old appearance intact.

Removing a finish may be accomplished several ways. The technique you use depends on the type of finish you're removing and whether you're only partially removing finish—for example, refinishing a badly damaged top when the rest of the piece is fine. Most folks jump right into it, only to find more work than they've bargained for. So, the project gets put off or taken to a professional to be completed. Few people would claim that stripping a finish is fun, but it can be bearable and efficient if you understand the materials that are used, and which strippers work best for the finish you're taking off.

Stripping can be done by mechanical means, with heat or with chemicals. Mechanical stripping entails the use of either sanding or scraping to remove the finish. This technique is best when you want to selectively remove finish. However, patina is lost so it's not

the best method if you're after limited restoration. It should be noted, though, that if your project is a table, desk, dresser or any furnishing with a broad surface that's in poor condition, you may want to use a belt sander to remove the finish, along with a thin layer of wood—called "resurfacing." Heat stripping involves using heat guns to remove finish and is a somewhat labor-intensive method of removing a finish. There's also the chance of scorching the wood or gouging it with a putty knife. The best use for heat guns is in stripping multiple layers of paint off of wood trim that you'd prefer not to remove. The most efficient method for stripping furniture, and the one which will cause the least amount of damage to the surface (such as removing patina or gouging the wood) is chemical stripping. Certain strippers work better on some finishes than others, so it helps if you know the type of finish that you have to take off. See page 73 for information on identifying a finish.

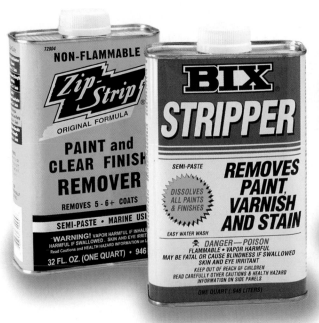

Methylene chloride strippers are highly effective products for removing just about any wood finish. They are by far the most commonly used paint stripping products, in part because they are relatively inexpensive. When using methylene chloride-based products, be sure to provide ample ventilation (using them outdoors is best) and to wear protective equipment.

Chemical stripping

Chemical strippers available today fall into five categories, based on the chemicals they contain. Manufacturers must list chemical components that are hazardous, so consumers can know exactly what they are buying. As a general rule, the level of hazard to you is an indicator of how efficient the stripper is, meaning how quickly it will work to remove a finish: that is, the nastier the substance the better it tends to work.

Consequently, one of the goals of chemical stripping is to determine what is the least caustic product that will be effective for your project. Even with mild chemical strippers, proper ventilation and protective wear are extremely important (See next page). Always read and follow the manufacturer's directions and recommendations for safe use of their product.

Methylene chloride. See photo, above. Methylene chloride has

been the main ingredient in strippers for decades. It is the fastest and most efficient stripper for removing all types of finishes. Two of its big advantages are that methylene chloride is non-flammable (some strippers are quite combustible), and it works from the "bottom up," meaning that it penetrates and swells the finish until it breaks free at the surface of the wood and can then be removed cleanly and easily.

CAUTION: Methylene chloride is a suspected carcinogen, and it evaporates very quickly, causing a rapid build-up of the vapors. Those fumes can rob anyone nearby of an adequate supply of oxygen. For that reason, people with heart problems are especially sensitive to such exposures and should not use methylene chloride strippers.

A typical methylene chloride-based stripper contains about 75% methylene chloride. The rest of the solution is composed of methyl alcohol to help the methylene chloride penetrate faster, detergents to wet the surface of the finish, activators like alkalis (ammonia or lye) and paraffin wax dissolved in

Multiple layers of old paint can be removed quickly and effectively with chemical strippers, particularly methylene chloride-based strippers. Methylene chloride actually begins working from the bottom layer of paint, making it possible to dissolve several layers in one application.

toluene to prevent the other solvents from evaporating too quickly. Other than masks that supply air from an outside source, no standard respirators are rated to handle methylene chloride fumes. So the best place to use it is outdoors or in a fully ventilated area.

MAT (Methanol, Acetone, Toluene). See page 110. These strippers are often sold as "refinishers," and they are effective only on lacquer and shellac finishes. Unlike methylene chloride, they work from the "top down" by dissolving the finish layer-by-layer. They are most effective when used with abrasive pads like steel wool. MAT strippers will not work very well on paint, and they have only a negligible effect on varnishes. Because they evaporate quickly, you must keep the surface saturated, or the stripper will evaporate, and the finish will re-harden on the wood. Sometimes MAT strippers contain a small amount of methylene chloride to give them some added kick. The downside with these strippers is that they are extremely flammable, so you must use them in a well-ventilated area and take the appropriate precautions. A cartridge style respirator will properly filter the vapors, except for any methylene chloride that's added.

NMP (N-methyl pyrrolidone). See page 111. This relative newcomer provides a safer alternative to methylene chloride-based strippers. The chemical is toxic, but the vapors build up less because the solution evaporates more slowly. This makes the stripper safer to use and keeps the surface wet—and active—longer. NMP is an expensive chemical to manufacture, so makers often add others, such as *d-limonene* (usually billed on the label as a "citrus scent"), *butyrolactone* and *dibasic esters.* NMP strippers work on all finishes, but they're sometimes double or triple the cost of other strippers.

Lye (Sodium hydroxide). See page 111. Lye will effectively remove multiple layers of oil and

Using chemical strippers safely

All strippers should be treated as hazardous materials, but some are more dangerous than others. Here are a few basic safety rules to follow when working with chemical strippers.

• Regarding the buildup of fumes, you can safely use NMP, DBE and lye-based strippers indoors, but methylene chloride and MAT's should only be applied outdoors or in a very well ventilated room.

• Goggles and gloves are a must with any stripper. Any chemical-resistant glove, like butyl or neoprene, is suitable for use with strippers except methylene chloride. There are only a few kinds of gloves that will provide protection against methylene chloride strippers for more than 30 minutes, but butyl or neoprene gloves will protect your skin as long as you avoid prolonged contact directly with the stripper.

• It's best to avoid direct contact with strippers, especially methylene chloride, so use a brush or putty knife to scrape off the finish and wear an apron and a long-sleeved shirt.

• A good vapor respirator will work with any stripper except methylene chloride.

• MAT strippers are extremely flammable, so take care to avoid using these near sparks or open flames.

• Of all the chemical ingredients in all of the strippers listed here, sodium hydroxide, or lye, is by far the most dangerous. The 30% to 40% concentration needed to strip paint is enough to blind you or eat the skin off your hand. Working with lye, you need to wear heavy-duty rubber gloves, an apron and goggles.

• And remember, any paint in the waste sludge that you remove may contain lead. You need to check your local hazardous waste codes to find out how to dispose of any stripping waste properly.

• Always read and follow the manufacturer's directions for safe use that are printed on the container.

casein (milk) paint. It's the main ingredient used in the large dip tanks of commercial refinishing shops. Unfortunately, it will discolor any tannin-rich wood (such as oak), and it will swell the fibers, resulting in a stringy surface if left on too long. However, it's cheap, and it's a good stripper for using on architectural millwork that will be repainted.

Sodium and ammonium hydroxide (lye and ammonia) are sometimes added to methylene chloride strippers to make them more effective on paint. The discoloration caused by the reaction with tannins can be difficult to remove, so avoid using these strippers—except as a last resort—on wood that will get a clear finish. And with lye in particular, you'll encounter a number of safety concerns. It's usually packaged in a gel or thick paste, and a supplied paper is applied over it to keep the water in it from evaporating.

Specialty tools for stripping furniture

In addition to the stripper itself, there are a few items you should have to make the finish removal task neater and more effective. *Dental picks* are handy for picking out paint from crevices, but in a pinch a sharpened piece of wood or a *nutpick* will work. *Brass brushes* are handy for removing paint lodged in large-pored woods, like oak. *Twine* can be used to clean up turned legs. If you have a planer, save the chips. They're great for removing stripper residue and can be worked with a bristle brush to remove stripping sludge from carvings and other intricate areas. *Putty knives* in various widths

are used to lift finish up off the wood once the stripper has softened it. Sand the sharp corners off lightly so they don't dig into the wood. *Steel wool* and synthetic steel wool *(Scotchbrite)* is handy. Finally, have plenty of rags and old newspapers on hand.

Preparing furniture for chemical stripping. Stripping is easier and more manageable if you can break down the furniture into smaller pieces before you start. Begin by removing all hardware, glass and mirror. Remove upholstery, take tops off (if they come off easily), along with removing backs and legs if you can. Its also advisable to do all repairs, like gluing breaks or replacing parts, before stripping. As long as the repair has good wood-to-wood contact, the glue joint won't be affected by the stripper.

Using chemical strippers. While methylene chloride stripper is the fastest-acting chemical stripper, the speed of any stripping agent is affected by temperature. So make sure the stripper, the piece you're stripping and the room are all within the range of comfortable room temperature. Although most strippers have a paste consistency and will cling, somewhat, to vertical surfaces, you're better off orienting the part you're stripping so it's flat. Brush the stripper on thickly with an old or inexpensive bristle brush. If the stripper comes with paper to lay over the stripper (like many NMP and lye strippers) place it over the stripper.

Methylene chloride will start to bubble the finish almost instantly (a sure sign it's working), but wait to start removing it until you can slip a putty knife under the finish and it peels off easily. The other types of chemical strippers don't bubble: the finish gets softened to the point where you can get the putty knife under it. When attempting to remove thick finishes and paint, several applications may be necessary, but a very general rule is to apply the stripper and then walk away and find something else to do. In other words, let the stripper do the work (but don't allow it to sit so long it dries out). On flat surfaces, remove as much of the stripper/finish residue as you can, using a putty knife. When using a putty knife, scrape off the blistered finish into a cardboard box or use the knife to transfer the stripper/finish by scraping the knife across the edge of the box. On curved surfaces, use 0 or 00 steel wool to remove the sludge. After removing all the sludge, use rags to wipe the wood as clean as possible. When the wood is clean, wash the residual stripper off with solvent. For methylene chloride and NMP strippers, use naphtha, mineral spirits or lacquer thinner to clean the surface. A nylon brush will help you get the wood clean. If small areas of finish remain, you can reapply stripper and repeat. Do not scrub the finish in a single area too much, or it will appear lighter than other areas when you finish it (assuming you're not going to sand much before applying finish). When stripping with lye, wash the working area with plenty of distilled water, followed by a rinse with white vinegar to neutralize the lye. NOTE: Lye (and strippers to which lye or ammonia have been added) will darken certain woods, particularly oak, cherry, mahogany and walnut. This darkening can be reversed with oxalic acid as explained in the section on bleaches (See pages 123 to 125).

Methylene-chloride and lye-stripped furniture is ready to finish in a day or so. NMP-stripped furniture will take longer to dry before you can apply finishing materials. That's because the solvents in NMP take longer to evaporate. Try to keep the furniture as warm as possible. The furniture is ready to finish when the wood feels dry to the

Remove hardware, glass and other nonwood furniture parts before you begin chemically stripping a piece of furniture. Store the removed items in a safe spot. It's often a good idea to label the parts so you know exactly where they came from.

touch and sands without the sandpaper clogging up. You can speed up the dry time by repeated rinsing with denatured alcohol.

Paint (and other problems). There are several problems with chemical stripping that occur on a fairly regular basis. One is with paint and the other is with intricate surfaces. Paint will remain in the pores of large-pored woods like oak unless the paint was applied over an existing clear finish. To get the paint out, try the following technique:

Remove as much of the paint as you can from the surface, then apply a generous coat of stripper and lay wax paper over it. Let it sit until you see the paint in the pores start to puff out. Then, use a brass-bristle brush to scrub the paint out. Stubborn paint can be picked out with a dental pick or nutpick. See page 109.

Intricate surfaces, like turned legs and carvings, can be cleaned of finish effectively by several means. One is to wrap a piece of

twine around the turned areas and pull the twine back and forth, shoe-shine style. This will gently abrade the finish off. You can also purchase abrasive sanding cord to accomplish the same thing. A sharpened piece of wood (use a pencil sharpener to put a point on a pencil-sized dowel) can be used to clean small crevices and detailed areas without damaging them. Planer shavings used with a nylon brush can clean up carved areas very effectively. If you don't have a planer, try asking a cabinet shop to part with some shavings.

Cleaning up. To dispose of the "sludge" when you're finished with it, it's perfectly safe to spread it out onto some newspapers layered up in a shallow box and place it outside. The solvents will evaporate (NMP will take longer than others). Eventually, you'll wind up with a dried, crusty residue. It's then safe to throw this out, but only if it's a clear finish. For paint (which may contain lead), call your local waste management agency.

1 Work in a very well ventilated area—preferably, outdoors. Wear protective gear (See page 103), including neoprene rubber gloves. Take care to avoid contact with the stripper. Using an old (or cheap disposable) bristle brush, apply a generous layer of stripper onto the surfaces. Brush in long strokes to avoid overworking the stripper. To help minimize contact with the stripper, pour small amounts into a metal container, refilling the container as necessary. Don't try to dip the brush into the original container, and never dump the stripper from the container onto the workpiece or try to apply the chemical directly from the container to the brush.

2 Allow the chemical stripper ample time to work. The finish surface will begin to bubble almost immediately, but wait until you can scrape the finish off cleanly and easily with a metal putty knife. The product container will likely suggest an amount of time to let the stripper work undisturbed. The photo to the right shows a chemically stripped finish that is ready to be scraped with a putty knife.

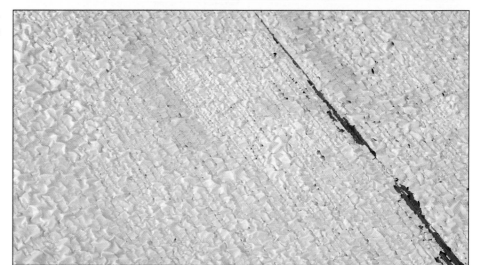

3 Use a broad metal putty knife (or wallboard taping knife) to remove the sludge from flat surfaces. Don't get too aggressive here, though. Strippers soften wood, so attempting to scrape off finish that has not been loosened can cause considerable damage to the wood. All you're doing at this point is shoveling up the sludge. Dispose of the sludge in a cardboard box lined with newspaper, cleaning off the knife on the edges of the box. If some of the finish did not come off, reapply stripper to that area, but be careful not to work it too much: this can cause it to lighten more than the rest of the wood. On curved surfaces, remove the sludge with steel wool. See page 108 for more finish removal tips.

4 Neutralize the chemical stripper by washing the surfaces down with the solvent recommended on the product label. Generally, mineral spirits, naphtha or denatured alcohol will be suggested. Use steel wool to wipe the surfaces. The steel wool will scrub additional sludge and finish out of wood pores.

5 Use a clean rag to thoroughly dry the wood surfaces. Inspect the rag. If you see evidence of old finish on the rag, re-wipe the surface with solvent and steel wool, then try drying with another clean rag. This may require a few repetitions. Be sure to clean out crevices and edges as well.

6 Allow the wood to dry for at least a day before sanding. Inspect the sandpaper (start with 100- or 150-grit) as you work. If it is gumming up, the wood hasn't dried adequately. Wait and try later.

Use common baling twine to rub finish residue and sludge out of crevices in rounded parts. Buff back and forth, as if you were shining a pair of shoes.

OPTION: Use abrasive sanding cords to remove finish residue from round crevices. Sanding cord is particularly useful after the finish and stripper have dried. If the material being removed is not completely dry, wear gloves.

Planer shavings can be dumped onto the surface after the chemical stripper has finished working. The shavings will soak up much of the stripper, making removal much neater.

Disposal tip: Dispose of the stripping sludge as you work, in a cardboard box lined with newspaper. Once you've removed all the sludge from the object being stripped, spread out the deposits in the box so they form a thin layer. This should be done outdoors. Let the chemicals in the sludge evaporate before disposing of the dried residue.

1 Finished surfaces are relatively easy to strip, but removing the last one percent of the finish from stubborn areas often takes as much, if not more, time than the other 99 percent. One of the favorite hiding places for stubborn finish is in the wood pores, especially on open-grained woods, like oak. To get these troublesome specks out, first brush a thin coat of chemical stripper over the entire surface. Then, lay wax paper over the area to keep the stripper from drying out. This extends the working time long enough for the stripper to penetrate into these areas.

2 Wait at least 30 minutes, then remove the wax paper. Scrub the surface with a brass-bristle brush: it may help to dip the brush in stripper first. This should dislodge most of the specks. Extra-stubborn finish can be removed with a dental pick or a nutpick, or even a piece of sharpened wood. Rinse the entire surface with stripper solvent (See container label) to neutralize it, then dry with a clean rag.

MAT strippers, usually called "furniture refinisher" by manufacturers, are intended to be used for partial finish removal only: to "revive" a finish by getting rid of the damaged or worn top layer. Most consist primarily of lacquer thinner. If used successfully, they can yield similar results to a complete stripping and refinishing, but with considerably less time and work. They are effective only on lacquer and shellac finishes.

Furniture refinisher (MAT)

Refinisher strippers (MAT strippers) are effective only on old shellac and lacquer finishes, so make sure you do the "tissue" finish test (See page 73) before using them. They're generally rubbed on with a medium-grade steel wool (00) but you can use a finer grade if you want to be less aggressive and try and preserve as much of the original color and patina of the finish as possible. Pour some of the stripper into a shallow pan, dunk the steel wool pad into it and saturate the finish. Scrub the stripper with the refinisher, working with the grain, which helps it to work faster. Continue until as much of the finish is removed as you want, then rinse with alcohol or lacquer thinner.

HOW TO REMOVE FINISH LAYERS WITH MAT STRIPPER

1 To remove the surface of a lacquer or shellac finish with finish refinisher, pour some of the product into a metal container then dab it onto the surface with 00 steel wool. Work the chemical evenly across the surface. Switch to clean pieces of steel wool frequently. Gauge the amount of finish being removed as you go, trying to maintain even surface coloration.

2 Work in logical sections: don't try to refinish the whole piece at once, but try to work within distinct borders. Once the finish has been removed to your satisfaction, wipe the surface with a clean rag dipped in the stripper solvent recommended on the container. Let the surface dry completely before touching/wiping it further: it will be tacky for some time.

N-methyl pyrrolidone (NMP) strippers

Often referred to as "safe strippers", N-methyl-pyrrolidone (NMP) strippers are a relatively new entry in the chemical stripper market. While the active ingredient in the products is toxic, NMP strippers contain retarders that slow down the rate of evaporation, decreasing the speed at which harmful vapors accumulate. This also prolongs the stripping activity, which is necessary since these types do not work as quickly as more aggressive products, like methylene chloride. The active time is further increased on some types by covering the stripper with plastic sheeting after it is applied. Covered, the strippers will continue to work for many hours, making them a popular choice for stripping woodwork. Although they are billed as "safe stripper," NMP products should be treated with the same safe handling practices as other chemical strippers.

Lye-based stripper

Lye (sodium hydroxide) is perhaps the oldest chemical stripper. It can cut through some old-style types of paint that other paint strippers will barely touch. It's also used frequently by professional and commercial stripping outfits in their large dipping tanks—mostly for reasons of economy, as it is relatively cheap. Because lye is a very caustic chemical, it is not recommended for general stripping use by do-it-yourselfers, with one exception: lye-based strippers are sometimes packaged as a gel or thick paste, and are supplied with protective paper that is applied over the chemical to keep it from evaporating. Generally, these products are used on large-scale home woodwork-stripping projects. The lye, however, can cause darkening and discoloration in some wood species.

Dutch Cupboard is No Treat

*Promising project teaches a
valuable (but expensive) lesson:
Don't let excitement cloud your judgment.*

One of the unavoidable truths about refinishing furniture is that you never really know what you've got until you're past the point of no return. Finishes can hide a multitude of sins, and

removing any finish is always taking a risk. This is an especially important point to learn well if you are engaging in furniture restoration for a profit.

Dutch cupboards, so-called because the basic design and

styling was developed by the Pennsylvania Dutch, are very collectible household furnishings. They are efficient users of space and have a spareness to their design and appearance, but with just enough nuances of flavor to keep them from being just another box. So when the Dutch cupboard you see pictured here showed up one day, we were interested. Excited, even. But it was in pretty rough shape, that was obvious. It had been painted and repainted within an inch of its life, and none of the layers seemed to be holding (this should have been a clue). The tabletop on the lower breakfront was missing its original countertop surface (a bad sign, as far as value goes). Some of the hardware was mismatched, doors were sagging, the glazing on the upper cabinet door was mysteriously painted over. But despite all these warning signs, we decided to tackle the project. The cupboard was just too charming to pass up, and the potential, if all went well, was high.

We began the project by disassembling as much of the cabinet as we could, making it easier to get at the various parts to make repairs and strip the finish. We removed the wooden cabinet doors and scraped off some of the loose paint. Surprise number one: From the back, where the wood was mostly visible, the doors looked fine. But on the faces of the doors, we found numerous wood plugs that went only partway into the panels. As we hoped to give the wood a natural finish, this was a setback.

But the real surprise came when we started trying to strip the finish. Methylene chloride wouldn't cut it. Lye had no effect. NMP stripper rolled off it like water off a duck. It refused to be scraped. In short, it proved to be indestructible. We carted a sample of the finish around to a few experts. Many guesses were made, but no one had seen anything quite like it before. Without knowing what we were dealing with, there was really no

The backs of these cabinet door looked just fine (top photo). Nice old pine, sturdy joinery, no discernible defects or major blemishes. But looks can be deceiving . . .

The cabinet fronts were another story altogether (bottom photo). We scraped off a bit of loose paint where we could and, to our great disappointment, we found that all of the faces were pockmarked with big wood plugs. There seemed to be no good reason for them. But our hopes for a beautiful, natural finish were quickly being dashed.

way to know how to get it off.

This setback left us only one option: Go down the auto parts store, pick up a few quarts of *Bondo* to fill in the chips and gaps in the surfaces, then paint the whole thing once again. Perhaps even with a faux finish, so it at least looked like wood.

We considered this option, but not for very long. By now, we had many hours of hard work and head scratching already invested in the Dutch cupboard, but the time to cut our losses seemed to be at hand. Besides, there was no

way of knowing if still more surprises would pop up as we continued. So we contacted the party we'd acquired the piece from and were able to make a deal to return it. But not a very favorable one.

In the end, we could only chalk it up to experience. "You never know what lies beneath the surface." As far as lessons go, it's a good one. Sometimes, perhaps, you do get what you pay for.

~MJ

Surface Preparation

Preparation of a wood surface for finish application involves two main activities: removing defects and smoothing and leveling the wood surface. In addition, the process includes elimination of minor defects like small dents, gouges and scratches. It is in the surface preparation that most unsuccessful refinishing projects fail. You've spent quite a bit of time already removing the finish and making repairs, so it's natural to try and hurry up a bit at this stage so you can get the new finish applied. The effects of hurrying, however, will be quite visible after the finish is applied. It is impossible to produce a professional-looking finish on a wood surface that is disfigured by sanding marks, rough surfaces, stains and other defects. So take your time in this vital area. Once the finish is applied, you'll be glad you did.

The two categories of

tools you'll need for most surface preparation are *scraping tools* and *abrasives.* Scrapers are ideal if you want to keep the production of dust to a minimum. There are many types of scrapers designed for a multitude of uses, but the type you're likely to use most frequently is the *cabinet scraper.* Cabinet scrapers, and any other scrapers, need to be very sharp to work correctly. Scrapers are filed flat, honed to 600 grit, then a burr is turned to produce a hook which removes fine, delicate shavings. Doing final smoothing of a wood surface with a cabinet scraper will yield a surface that accepts finish evenly and feels "authentic" because it was achieved using the same methods our ancestors used for working wood (this makes scraping an excellent choice for readying an antique).

Abrasives are available in a wide variety of shapes, styles and forms, from flat sheets of paper to cushioned pads. Three different types, designated by the type of

Limited restoration

When you want to preserve as much of the original surface color and patina as possible, forgo most of the sanding and scraping process. However, sanding is a good way to clean the wood so finishing materials adhere, so you'll want to do a light sanding with 180-grit sandpaper. Tear a sheet into quarters, then take one of the quartered sheets and fold it into thirds so that no abrasive touches abrasive. Using your hand to back up the paper, sand the wood using light pressure.

Steaming out dents

Dents are simply depressions caused by compressed wood fibers. As long as the wood fibers have not been severed, they can be swelled to level with heat and water. Drop some distilled water into the dent and cover it with a wet cloth (use distilled water on the cloth too). With a household iron set on high, place the tip of it on the cloth over the dent for a few seconds. Remove it, then repeat. Pull back the cloth to see if the dent has swelled back up, and re-wet it and repeat the process until it comes up to the surface, or at least close to it. Don't leave the iron on for more than five seconds. When the surface has dried, a light sanding with 180- or 220-grit sandpaper is all that's needed to blend the area that you worked on with the rest.

abrasive, are used in finishing. *Garnet,* a natural mineral, is used for hand-sanding applications and is available only in sheets. *Aluminum oxide,* a man-made abrasive, is available in a wider variety of styles and is used for hand- or machine-sanding. It's tougher than garnet and breaks as you use it, exposing fresh cutting edges so it lasts longer than garnet. *Silicon carbide* is also man-made and is tougher than aluminum oxide. It shows up in a wide variety of forms, but the most familiar type is the black or grayish-colored wet/dry sandpaper that's used in between coats of finish and rubbing the finish out. It's used with a lubricant—typically water, but mineral spirits can also be used.

Surface repairs. Sanding alone may not remove all the defects from the surface. If the surface is otherwise in good shape, except for a small dent or gouge, and you don't want to disturb the patina by sanding the wood, you'll have to fill in the defect or steam it out. Steaming dents is accomplished with an ordinary household iron (See *Steaming out dents,* above). Filling is normally done with wood putty (although sometimes auto body filler may be used).

1 Sand all the surfaces to remove any last traces of the old finish and knock down any raised grain, splinters or rough edges. See pages 116 to 121.

2 Fill gouges and surface defects with wood putty, if they can't be removed using other methods. See page 122.

3 Get rid of stains or discoloration in the wood. See pages 123 to 125. Finish-sand the surfaces and wipe clean with a tack cloth before applying the finish materials.

Scraping wood surfaces

Cabinet scrapers are common finishing tools in fine wood shops, but given their utility and ease of use, they should be more widely known than they are. For smoothing wood surfaces, they simply can't be beat. Sandpaper is slow, messy and leaves fine scratches. A cabinet scraper, when sharpened and used correctly, takes shavings like a plane, but thinner and across a wider surface. And, it won't cause tearout—even on a burl. Unlike sandpaper, which requires you to work through numerous grits to progress from rapid stock removal to a fine surface finish, a scraper cuts quickly and leaves a finished surface.

Scrapers are comfortable doing everything from crude work to the very finest woodcrafting. A few tasks they're often used for include smoothing a surface before fine sanding, scraping off dried glue, and even smoothing and dressing a lacquer or varnish finish. The scraper also excels at flushing up inlays and leveling high spots.

Burnishing option

Freehand burnishing. Hold the scraper vertically, pushing one corner into a workbench, while flexing the scraper into a gradual curve. Burnish the edge with firm strokes down the edge, holding the burnisher slightly less than 90° to the face. Flex the scraper in the other direction to raise a burr on the opposite edge.

HOW TO CREATE A SMOOTH SURFACE WITH A CABINET SCRAPER

1 To use a hand scraper, hold it so that your two thumbs are in the middle of the scraper and wrap your other fingers around the other side. Flex the scraper with your thumbs, pushing outward, and tilt it forward to an approximate 45° angle. Push the scraper away from your body and downward slightly so a small whisker-thin shaving is produced. You can change the angle slightly up or down to change the "bite" of the scraper.

2 Once you get the hang of it, you can try pulling the scraper toward your body. The scraper will dull as you use it, and you'll know this when it produces dust, not thin shavings. Since you have four cutting edges or burrs, just use a different edge. When you've used up all four edges, re-sharpen it (See next page).

HOW TO SHARPEN A CABINET SCRAPER

1 Remove remnants of the old burr. Lay the scraper on a flat surface and use a fine, single-cut mill file to shear off traces of the old burr. Hold the file nearly flat across the face of the scraper and work gently. A few broad strokes are all you should need to flatten the faces along the edges.

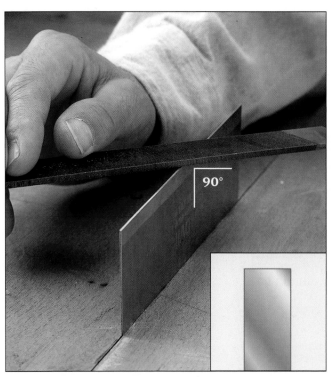

2 Square and smooth the edges. Clamp the scraper vertically in a vise and run a mill file along the edge, holding the file diagonally to the length of the scraper and perpendicular to the face. Your goal here is to flatten the edges lengthwise and square them to the faces (See inset).

3 Raise the new burrs. Set the scraper flat on the workbench and close to a side. Lay the burnisher across the scraper and against an edge, tipping the burnisher over the edge of the bench a couple of degrees down from horizontal. Stroke firmly along the edge of the face, back and forth a few times to raise a burr along each edge (See inset).

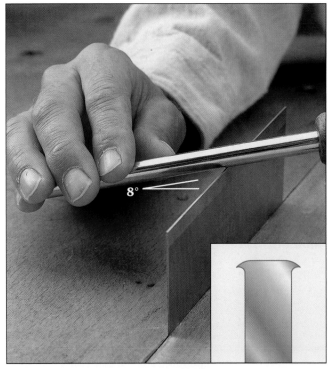

4 Turn the burrs. Clamp the scraper vertically in a vise and run the burnisher along the raised edge, about 8° down from horizontal. When done, you should be able to feel the burr evenly along the edge by running a finger across the face and over the edge (See inset).

Emery
cloth for
metal and
plastics

40-grit
aluminum
oxide

100-grit
aluminum
oxide

220-grit
aluminum
oxide

400-grit
wet/dry

Sandpaper grit chart

Grit number	Description	Use
12 16 20 24	Very Coarse	Very rough work requiring high speed, heavy machinery. Used for unplaned woods, uneven wood floors and rough-cut lumber.
30 36 40 50	Coarse	Rough carpentry.
60 80 100	Medium	General carpentry.
120 150 180	Fine	Preparation of hardwoods and final smoothing of softwoods.
220 240 280	Very Fine	Final and between-coat sanding. Used to remove sanding marks left by coarser grits.
320 360 400	Extra Fine	Sanding between finish coats and wet-sanding paints and varnishes.
500 600	Super Fine	Sanding metal, plastics, ceramics and wet-sanding.

Sandpaper & sanding

Whether you sand by hand or machine, the goal is the same. You level the surface with coarse grits and then move on up to finer grits to smooth the surface. 80- or 100-grit is a good place to start, but only if there are big scratches, dents or other defects. The general idea is that you work the surface with the sandpaper until the marks are removed and the surface is level. Then you switch to a higher grit (around 150 or so) and sand until the previous, deeper scratches are removed. If you have trouble seeing if you have removed them successfully, position a light directly behind the surface at the same level. Then, switch to 220-grit. Wiping the surface with mineral spirits when you're finished will highlight any spots you missed, and you can touch these up by returning to a lower grit. Remember, if there's only minimal damage to the surface of the wood, you can start with 120- or 150-grit.

Most woodworkers have problems with sanding. They either sand way too much (and to too high a grit) or they are sloppy and don't level the wood well enough, missing complete areas of the surface. Here are a few tips to help you know how much to sand:

• If the surface has damage, like scratches or small gouges, level it first using 80- or 100-grit. Start sanding diagonally at roughly a 35° to 45° angle. If you're sanding by hand, tear the sandpaper into quarters and wrap it around a cork, rubber or soft wooden block. This levels the surface more efficiently than sanding with the grain. After several passes across the entire width, switch to the opposite angle and repeat. Then, finish with the grain until all the defects are removed.

• Switch to the next grit (120) and sand with the grain until all the scratches from the previous grit are gone. Then go on up to 150, 180, then finally 220.

• In most cases, sanding to 220-grit is fine if you plan on using a hard finish like shellac, lacquer or varnish. The only time you should sand finer than 220 is when using "in-the-wood" penetrating finishes. There's a subtle luster difference when you sand beyond 220 and as far up as 400 or 600. It's a lot of extra work, so you'll have to try it and see if it's worth the extra labor.

Sanding Tools

Sanding blocks. Occasional contour work can be done with a folded sheet in the bare hand, but hand-sanding is generally done with some kind of sanding block or pad. There are all sorts of fancy sanding block contraptions out there, but a simple wood or cork block is the easiest to use, cheapest, and most comfortable. The common rounded-top solid cork block is fine, or you can make one up from a block of wood, $4\frac{1}{2} \times 2\frac{1}{2} \times 1\frac{1}{2}$ in. high, with a $\frac{1}{8}$-in.-thick cork sheet glued to the bottom, and all top corners rounded over. A half-sheet sander, made twice as long and used sideways, is even better for leveling imperfections when you're applying a reflective finish that will magnify any distortions. Wood alone can be used for a block, but it tends to wear the paper more quickly. Hard felt, cork or rubber on the bottom works better. To tear sandpaper to size, fold it, then tear along the sharp edge of a tabletop or a hacksaw blade.

Contour sanding. For sanding contours, flexible foam pads work well. Contour sanding grip sets include a variety of foam rubber shapes (convex, concave and angles) that you can wrap a piece of sandpaper around.

There are even sandpaper devices made just to ease sanding tiny grooves, beads and routed surfaces. Abrasive cords and tapes will get into narrow scroll saw kerfs and fine details on wood or metal. Sanding sticks are miniature manual belt sanders with pointed noses to get them into tight situations.

HAND SANDERS & SANDING BLOCKS

Commercial sanding block

Sanding sponges

"Tear-drop" sanding blocks

PORTABLE POWER SANDERS

3 × 24 belt sander

Random-orbit sander

Detail sander

Finishing sander (¼ sheet)

Remove sawdust with a soft-bristled brush or by blowing with compressed air. Then, use a tack cloth to give the wood surfaces a thorough cleaning. Even if you're working in a dedicated clean room for finishing, wipe the surfaces with a tack cloth again if you wait more than a few minutes before applying the finishing products.

3 steps to perfect sanding

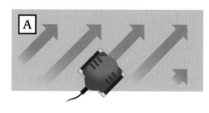

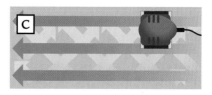

Start sanding diagonally at roughly a 35 to 45° angle to the grain with 80- or 100-grit sandpaper (A). This levels the wood surface more efficiently than sanding with the grain. Once you've sanded the entire surface, switch to the opposite angle and repeat (B). Finish leveling the surface by sanding with the grain (C). Switch to 150-grit sandpaper and sand with the grain until all the scratches from the previous grit are gone. Remove any remaining scratches with 220-grit paper, sanding with the grain.

Sandpaper is difficult to tear in a straight line, and cutting it with scissors or a utility knife will dull blades very quickly. Build yourself a sandpaper cutter by attaching a hacksaw blade to a piece of scrap wood, with the sharp edge of the blade facing toward the edge of the board. Attach a strip of wood parallel to the blade. Position the strip so it's the same distance from the cutting edge of the blade as the most common dimension you'll need to fit your pad sander. Slip a piece of sandpaper underneath the blade and up against the strip. Pull upward against the blade for a neat cut.

A do-it-yourself sanding block made from a 1½ × 2½ × 4½-in. piece of scrap wood is a perfect fit for quarter-sheets of sandpaper. A piece of ⅛-in.-thick cork glued to the bottom provides cushion and helps preserve the life of the sandpaper sheet.

Power sanding tips

Orbital pad sander

Random-orbit sander

Random-orbit sanders vs. pad sanders. The shape of the sanding patterns created by orbital and random-orbit sanders is the main difference between the tools. With orbital sanders, the individual grits move in tight regular circles more likely to leave noticeable sanding marks than the sporadic, non-repeating grit marks of the random-orbit sander.

Sanding small parts. Decorative wood appliqués and small wood parts are easier to sand on a stationary sander. If you don't have one, you can convert your belt sander into a stationary sanding station by mounting the sander in a bench-mounted inversion stand.

A sanding station with a disc sander and a belt sander is a great investment if you plan on doing a lot of furniture work. By using the miter gauge and sanding table, you can use the sanding surfaces to trim parts to precise angles for a perfect fit.

Wood Putty

Wood putty is used to fill gouges or dents that won't steam out to level. It is sold in oil-based, water-based or solvent-based formulations. Normally, it comes as a pre-mixed paste or dough (it's sometimes called *wood dough*), but you can also find dry varieties that you mix with water or another component before application. Water-based putty is the most common and most people find it the easiest to use. The trick with putty is to apply it only to the defect: if it gets into open pores on surrounding wood it's hard to remove and will be visible once a finish is applied. To get around this problem, mask off the defect and apply the putty with a putty knife or screwdriver. Remove the tape, which will leave the putty slightly higher, which is fine because it will shrink slightly. When it's dry, sand it level.

Tips for working with wood putty

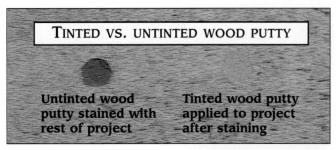

TINTED VS. UNTINTED WOOD PUTTY

Untinted wood putty stained with rest of project

Tinted wood putty applied to project after staining

The best method to conceal nail and screw heads with wood putty has been debated for generations. Try filling holes with putty tinted to match the finished color of the surrounding wood, rather than applying untinted putty first, then staining. Untinted putty may absorb more stain than the surrounding wood, making the repairs conspicuous.

Apply wood putty with a putty knife or an old slotted screwdriver. Take care to keep putty confined to the repair area only. Apply the putty until its surface is slightly higher than the surrounding wood. Allow the putty to dry thoroughly, then sand it flat.

Fill nail and screw holes, voids in plywood edges, and other surface defects with paintable or stainable wood putty. Overfill the area slightly, then sand the putty so it's even with the surface of the adjoining wood once the putty has dried.

Bleaching products useful in preparing a wood surface for a finish include: household chlorine bleach, for lightening certain wood stains; Oxalic acid, for selectively removing darker wood stains without affecting the surrounding wood; and two-part (A/B) alkali/peroxide wood bleach, for overall lightening of wood tones.

Bleaching wood

Bleaches have a number of uses in furniture refinishing. They can lighten a wood's natural color, remove certain stains and fix some problems that arise in the finishing process. There are three primary bleaching products that you can use. It's important to select the correct one because one product will not work in all situations. The three types are *alkali/peroxide bleach* (commonly sold as two-part bleach), *chlorine bleach* and *oxalic acid*.

Alkali/peroxide bleach. Also called A/B bleach, this two-part bleaching process removes the wood's natural coloring and establishes an even, off-white neutral base which may be desirable for certain finishes, like blonde mahogany. They can also be used to even out sapwood/heartwood color differences. They tend to rob wood of its depth and luster, so they should be used with discretion. To use this bleach, you apply solution A, and while it's still wet, you apply solution B. A slight foaming action tells you the bleach is working, but the full effect may not take place for several hours, so it's generally best to leave it overnight. A second application may be used if necessary. These bleaches are neutralized after drying by wetting the wood with a solution of equal parts white vinegar and water.

Chlorine bleach. This supermarket-variety, household bleach is used to remove dye stains and some miscellaneous stains, like grape juice and tea, from bare wood. The bleaching agent in these products is dilute *sodium hypochlorite.* It will work on dye-based stains, but several applications may be necessary because of its lack of strength and the fact that pre-mixed bleaches gradually lose their effectiveness sitting in a bottle on the store shelf. A better solution is to go to a swimming pool supply store and purchase a small bag of "shock treatment," which normally consists of calcium hypochlorite powder. This powder, when mixed with water at a rate of one tablespoon per cup, will yield a concentrated bleach that works much faster. Apply the bleach and let it sit overnight. Neutralize it with white vinegar.

Oxalic acid. The best reason to use oxalic acid on wood stains is its selectivity. It will remove iron-based stains (like those that appear around nails), black water stains and some other mishaps, without altering the natural color of the surrounding wood. Oxalic acid will also tone down the dark appearance of stripped and weathered wood (which is why it is a common ingredient in deck cleaners and brighteners). Oxalic acid is usually purchased as a dry powder or in crystalline form. It is mixed with hot water until the water is saturated and won't dissolve additional product. It is applied to the entire wood surface, not just to the stain. It may take several applications with several hours drying time in between to get the stain out. It's neutralized afterward with a solution of several tablespoons baking soda dissolved in warm water.

Selection chart for bleaching wood

IF YOU WANT TO:	USE:	NEUTRALIZE WITH:
Lighten up or remove natural color of wood	A/B Bleach	Water, then white vinegar (1 part vinegar to 2 parts water)
Remove dye stains	Chlorine bleach	2 to 3 applications of distilled water
Remove iron stains	Oxalic acid	2 applications distilled water followed by baking soda dissolved in water*
Lighten up stripped wood	Oxalic acid	2 applications distilled water followed by baking soda dissolved in water*
Remove water stains	Oxalic acid	2 applications distilled water followed by baking soda dissolved in water*

* Dissolve two tablespoons baking soda in a half-pint of hot water.
NOTE: If a stain is unknown, try oxalic acid first, then chlorine bleach second. Always wash the first bleach off completely before applying the second.

HOW TO REMOVE BLACK WATER STAINS

1 Prepare a mixture of oxalic acid solution. The standard technique is to start with a cup or so of hot water, then slowly add oxalic acid powder or crystals until they no longer dissolve. Brush the solution over the entire affected area—not just onto the black water stain. Be sure to read the "safe use" instructions on the container.

2 Allow the wood bleach sufficient time to work—often, leaving it overnight may be required. Additional applications may also be required if the stain does not disappear completely after the first treatment. When you're done, add two tablespoons of baking powder to a half-pint of distilled water and sponge the solution onto the surface to neutralize the bleach.

How to lighten wood tone with two-part (A/B) wood bleach

1 If you want to lighten the natural color of wood or reverse overall darkening that may have occurred, use two-part wood bleach (also called A/B bleach or alkali/peroxide bleach). The directions on the container generally suggest that you mix equal parts (A and B) from each container together in a separate container, then sponge the solution on. Many pro's, however, prefer to sponge on first the "A," then the "B." This allows better control of the amounts and reduces waste. Use either method to blend the bleaches.

2 Wearing heavy (preferably, neoprene) gloves, work the bleach or bleach solution into the wood. Spread it nice and evenly with a sponge. In most cases, the wood will begin to foam almost instantly. Let the bleach work until the color has lightened to your satisfaction. This may require you to reapply the solution, perhaps several times.

3 When the desired color tone has been achieved, wipe down the wood with a mixture of equal parts white vinegar and water. This will neutralize the lightening effects of the bleach. After the surface has dried thoroughly, sand it lightly to knock down any wood grain raised by the moisture.

BEFORE

AFTER

Tired Table Gets Minor Cosmetic Surgery

A brand new foot and a fine finish give this mahogany accent table a dramatic facelift.

A furniture restoration project doesn't need to take an enormous investment to provide a big payback. In fact, the return on investment we got from this small pedestal table would put any of the major market indexes to shame. It helps, of course, if there is very little wrong with the piece to begin with. And that was definitely the case with this project.

The most obvious issue that needed attention when we started work on this table was the "club" foot. One leg had splintered at the end, neatly shearing off the end of the part. And the missing piece, along with the decorative metal cap that covered it, were long gone. So our first challenge was to re-shoe the leg. We found a small piece of red mahogany that was similar in figure to the table legs, then planed the piece down so it was just slightly thicker than the full width of the leg (luckily, there were three good legs to serve as guides). We traced the outline of one of the good legs into the new material, then cut out the replacement foot on the band saw. After grafting the new foot onto the old leg with a scarf joint, we refined the shape by

Three of the table legs were still in perfect shape, so we used one to trace a replacement piece onto a piece of mahogany. We cut out the piece (slightly oversized) then trimmed it to form a scarf joint with the broken end of the leg.

After the patch piece was glued to the old leg, we shaped, contoured and carved it to match. This is almost always easier to do after the patch piece has been well bonded to the furniture.

cutting and carving until the foot matched its three counterparts.

The finish was in reasonably good shape, except for the tabletop. So we completely stripped and sanded the top down to bare wood. We used MAT stripper to remove only the top surface of the finish on the rest of the piece, however. A little touch-up and a fresh coat of lacquer, and the base looked as good as new. We stained the tabletop to match, then wiped on a grain filler to deepen the finish. Finally, we found a set of brass toe caps in a hardware supply catalog to give the table just the finishing touch it needed to really sparkle.

~MJ

Skills used in this project:

• *Making replacement parts (pages 56 to 57)*

• *Scarf joints (page 60)*

• *Using furniture refinisher (page 110*

• *Filling wood grain (pages 137 to 139)*

• *Finishing wood (pages 141 to 155)*

We stripped, sanded and refinished the tabletop, but were able to get by with only a limited restoration and some touch-up on the table base. A coat of grain filler made the new top surface glass-smooth. We got lucky and found a set of four replacement caps for the feet in a hardware catalog.

Applying a Finish

The finish is made up of one to three or four layers of material, each with a specific function. Depending on which products you use and what your goals are, the finish can provide color, depth, a shiny gloss and protection against moisture and sunlight. The ability to apply a smooth, professional-looking finish takes some practice and quite a bit of patience. But, on the plus side, it does not take a large investment of money, requiring only minimal tools to produce good results. Most of these tools are quite low in cost and are easily obtainable.

Applying a finish on furniture is essentially a five-step process:
1. Smooth and level wood surfaces.
2. Color the wood with stain.
3. Fill the wood pores.
4. Apply a finish (topcoat), sanding between coats.
5. Rub out the finish.

Before you begin any finishing task, here are a few general introductory tips to keep in mind: First, work in an orderly and logical manner in a clean, dry and warm environment. Finishing products perform best when applied between 65° and 75°F. Both the finish and the project should be at room temperature for best results.

Second, follow product application instructions carefully, especially suggested drying times. Shortening the drying time causes all sorts of problems. Some finishes will take even longer to dry in cold or damp environments, so be patient between coats.

Third, practice on samples. Apply the stain and top-coat you've chosen to actual cutoffs from your project lumber. This way you'll know exactly how the finish influences the color and grain pattern of the wood. The larger your samples are, the better.

Finally, work safely. Most finishes are hazardous. They may be flammable, toxic if swallowed, harmful to breathe or a skin irritant. Wear gloves, protective clothing, a respirator approved for fumes and safety glasses.

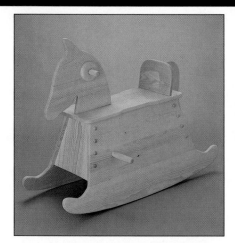

Polyurethane varnish is perhaps the most durable finish material, making it a good choice for pieces that will get a real workout.

Spray-on lacquer works nicely on furniture with flat surfaces and is consistent in appearance with more contemporary furnishings.

Clear shellac (amber) over uncolored pine is a traditional finish that will mellow with age.

Rich woods, like the white oak and walnut seen here, do nicely with a true oil finish or an oil/varnish blend.

Medium-tone stain gives depth and color to uninteresting wood (alder is seen here). Finished with renewable butcher block oil.

Dark-tinted grain filler gives richness, luster and a smooth surface to these nesting tables.

Paint is often overlooked as a furniture finishing option, but has many benefits you won't get from clear finishes (hiding defects is just one).

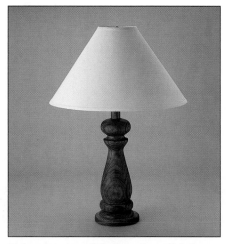

Plain paste wax will buff to a beautiful, deep gloss that is especially striking when used with a dark wood stain.

Deep-toned stain with a high-gloss finish is a traditional treatment for more formal furnishings.

Options for applying a finish

There are four basic options for applying finishing materials: brushes, rags and cloths, pads and rollers, and spray equipment.

Brushes. Paintbrushes are divided into two groups: *natural* and *synthetic.* Natural bristle brushes are commonly made from Chinese hogs (called China bristle brushes) and can be used with oils and oil-based products like varnish, shellac and lacquer. Synthetic bristle brushes are made from man-made fibers like nylon or polyester and are used for application of water-based products, but can also be used with most other finishes. It's a good idea to have at least one of each type. Natural bristle brushes tend to be better for flowing finishes like varnish and solvent lacquer.

Parts of a brush. The key features of a brush that determine its performance are *bristle shape* and *profile.* Bristles, both natural and synthetic, can be blunt-tipped, tapered or flagged (the bristle has splits at the end). They can also be a combination of these types. Blunt-tipped bristles are found mostly on cheap synthetic and natural bristle brushes. The end of the brush is blunt and squared off, which is bad for applying clear finishes (it leaves large ridges) but not necessarily a bad thing for working thick paints into the crevices of exterior wood. Some synthetics incorporate a taper and/or a flag at the end like natural bristle. This natural attribute results in the ability to produce a fine, smooth finish with larger brushes as well as smaller ones. The profile, or overall shape, is built into the brush during the brush-making process.

Brushes and applicators for applying finishes include: (A) disposable foam brush will work for water-based finishes but isn't the best option; (B) synthetic bristle brush, a better choice for applying water-based products, including paint; (C) and (D) natural bristle brushes for applying oil-based finishes, lacquer and shellac; (E) painting pad for applying paint to broad surfaces.

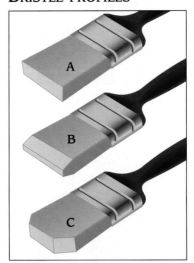

Lint-free paper toweling and rags are used to apply wipe-on finishing products. You can find them at paint stores, woodworking stores, and some building centers and hardware stores.

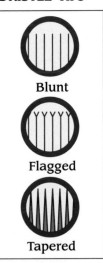

BRISTLE PROFILES

A

B

C

BRISTLE TIPS

Blunt

Flagged

Tapered

Bristle profile and tip shape determine brush performance to a large extent. *Flat profiles* (A) are a bad choice for applying clear finishes because they leave large ridges. Save these brushes for applying stains and paints. Chisel-tip brushes have shorter bristles on the outside and longer bristles in the center. Chiseled bristles are available in *rectangular* (B) or *round* (C) profiles. The chisel tip does a better job of laying down a smooth finish than flat profiles. Bristle tips can be blunt, flagged (bristles have splits at the ends), tapered or a combination of several shapes. Blunt tips, a sign of a cheap brush, tend to leave brush lines in the finish. Better brushes have flagged or tapered tips, which lay down fine, smooth finishes, regardless of brush size.

Good brushes are always made by hand and have different bristle lengths within a single brush. The positioning and thickness of the bristles can be used to create brushes that have different shapes for different uses. Chisel-tip brushes are handmade with shorter bristle lengths on the outside and longer bristles in the center. The chisel-tip does a better job of putting down a smooth finish than non-chiseled brushes. These brushes may be available with a rectangular profile or a round profile. The round profile uses approximately twice the number of bristles and is preferred by some because they hold much more material than other brushes.

Rags and cloths. Any natural-fiber, clean and absorbent material works for application of stains, but when it comes to finishes, the cloth should be as lint free as possible. Non-textured paper towels work very well for application of most oils and varnishes. A good alternative is to use old cotton garments, such as T-shirts.

Pads and rollers. Rollers work well for paint, but rarely are they suitable for application of clear finishes. For finish products, short-nap rectangular pads are a good choice for application to large, flat surfaces. Foam pads are also suitable for most varnishes and water-based finishes.

Spray equipment. Spray equipment that runs off a small turbine or a compressor is available at low cost these days. To minimize overspray, the purchase of HVLP (high volume/low pressure) equipment is suggested—rather than typical air-compressor-driven paint guns, which are hard to control and produce large amounts of overspray. Good results can be obtained with a surprisingly small investment in HVLP equipment. Spray equipment speeds things up quite a bit, especially on complicated pieces, and allows options for subtle techniques, like toning.

Professional finishing shops

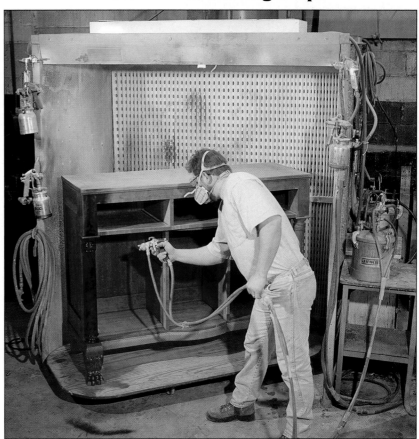

Where stripping a finish strikes some as a disagreeable process, applying a new finish makes many people nervous. After all, your work will be out there for everyone to see for many years. If you feel anxiety about finishing your furniture project yourself, there is always the professional option. Pros generally use air sprayers to apply extremely smooth, even finishes efficiently. Lacquer is a popular finish material, as it dispenses well with spray equipment. But advances in water-based finishes are making more options available. Many professionals also offer hand-applied finishing services.

HVLP sprayers (high volume, low pressure) have taken the home shop by storm in recent years. With internal turbines that deliver a lighter, more manageable spray, they are less prone to overspray and a bit more forgiving than compressor-driven spray guns. See pages 150 to 155.

Staining wood

Stains are liquids that give color to wood, yet still allow the wood grain and figure to show. Consumers often have a lot of difficulty choosing an appropriate stain because there are so many staining products on the market, each making its own claims. To better understand stain, and thereby enable yourself to make good purchasing choices, it's useful to first divide stains into two distinct groups: pigment stains and dye stains.

Pigment stains are composed of three ingredients: a dry, colored powder; a thinner (or carrier) that liquifies the powder so it can be applied to the wood; and a binder—a resin that envelopes the pigment so it can stick to the wood surface. Colored pigment is either a natural product mined from the earth (something like colored dirt), or a man-made powder such as lamp-black. Thinner is a liquid that's compatible with the binder, and may be solvent-based or water-based. Binder is a finish product, such as linseed oil, varnish or water-based resin.

Dye stains. Most pigment particles are large enough to be seen with a magnifying glass. On the other hand, dye is a powder that is dissolved into a liquid, and the resulting molecular solution contains colored particles thousands of times smaller than a pigment particle. The liquid that's used to dissolve the dye is called the carrier. It may be water- alcohol- or mineral spirit-

To stain or not to stain?

Everyone who has an opinion about furniture likely has an opinion about staining. To some, coloring wood is as natural as putting ketchup on French fries. To others, it is a sin against nature. It really is a matter of personal preference. But in case you are riding the fence between French fries and sin, here are a few pros and cons for each point of view.

Wood stains, when used judiciously, actually enhance the beauty of the wood. They subtly highlight the figure and the grain, drawing the eye to the best features of the wood. They can also lend a "mood" to wood, especially wood that's not too interesting to start with. A birch cabinet, for example, will look stark and contemporary if finished unstained. But if you apply some red mahogany stain prior to finishing, you'll swear the piece is really mahogany, with all the richness and luster the species is valued for.

On the other hand, wood stains can also detract from appearance by bombarding the eye with strong color at the expense of subtle figure.

The three identical nightstands shown here give a good indication of how the finished appearance of a piece of furniture is affected by wood stain. The best advice: Go with whatever you like most.

Finish only

based. The most important difference between a dye stain and a pigment stain is that dye has no binder and is a true solution (like salt in water), while a pigment stain is simply a suspension or mixture.

The differences between pigment and dye stains are important only to chemists and trivia buffs. They color wood differently. Pigment stains react to surface texture on different woods. Oak, ash, walnut, mahogany and any wood with open grain or pores reacts differently to a pigment stain because the pores act as traps for pigment. The pores color darker than the flat grain in between. Close-grained, dense wood like hard maple is difficult to stain with pigment because there's nowhere for the pigment to go. Because dye stain is molecular, it imparts an even color to hard, dense woods. As a general rule, open-pored woods look better with pigment stains and hard, dense woods look better with dye stains. Because of this, some manufacturers use both dye and pigment in the same product so the stain gives you the best of both worlds.

Pigment stains are the most common type of stain found in hardware stores and building centers. Dye stains can be purchased at paint stores and woodworking stores, in both pre-mixed and powder forms. The powder is mixed with your solvent of choice just before the stain is applied. Dye stains are usually indicated as such on the label or are sold as NGR (non-grain-raising) stains. If the can does not specifically say dye somewhere, it's probably a pigment stain or pig-

PIGMENT AND DYE STAINS

Pigment and dye stains color wood differently. Notice in the pigment-stained sample (left) how the porous wood grain is darker than the surrounding flat grain. The contrast between the pores and flat grain is more subtle in the dye-stained sample (right), because the dye penetrates the porous and flat-grained areas evenly.

ment/dye combination. In either case, the application method is similar.

Light stain with finish

Dark stain with finish

Applying stains. Regardless of type, apply wood stain quickly over the entire surface, then wipe the excess off with a clean rag. Be mindful of the amount of open time (the time you have before the stain starts to dry) you have to work the stain. Oil-based products evaporate more slowly than water- or alcohol-based products, affording you plenty of time to apply the stain and wipe it off evenly. That's why oil-based stains are the most popular.

The goal of staining is to produce an even tone that's precisely the color you want. As long as the stain has not dried, you can manipulate it as you please until it is the color you want.

• To lighten the stain, apply the solvent for the stain before it's cured. If it's still too dark, scrub it with some fine synthetic steel wool and solvent.

• To darken a stain, use a darker colored stain. If you're using a dye that you mixed, make a stronger

All stains are designed to color wood, but how well they perform on your project depends on which category of stain you use. Pigment stains, the most common variety you'll find in home centers and hardware stores, are best suited for woods like oak, ash and walnut, with large pores and open grain that trap the stain pigment. Dye stains are sold premixed or as concentrated dye powder that you mix with water or alcohol. They are better suited for tight-grained woods like maple, which cannot trap pigment as well. When it comes to identifying stain categories, product labels can be confusing, so test a stain on scrap before committing it to your project (See below).

Pigment stains

Dye stains

Test stains on a sample board to get an accurate idea of how they will look on your furniture. Presuming that you plan to apply a finish over the stain, you'll get the most accurate reading while the stain is still wet. Where possible, choose a sample board of the same wood species as your project (the plywood shown here has an oak veneer surface, which reacts very similarly to solid oak). And don't be shy about bringing a sample board to the store where you plan to purchase the stain. Many retailers will give you permission to test stains out before you make your purchase.

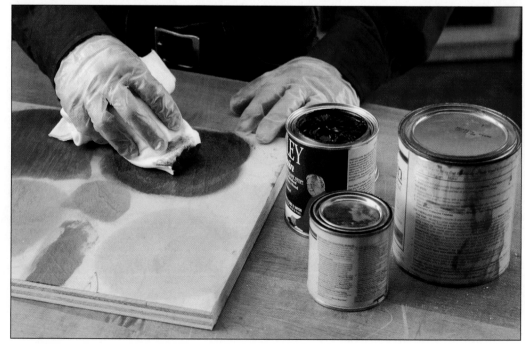

dye solution by adding more dye.

• To change the color, apply a different colored stain over the first stain while it's still wet.

The number one problem with staining is a condition known as blotching. Certain woods (notably, softwoods like pine, but also some hardwoods like cherry, poplar and soft maple) will stain unevenly due to variations in density at the wood surface. There are three workable solutions to the blotching problem.

1. Use a gel stain. Gel stains are thick, pigmented stains with lower solvent amounts, so they don't penetrate too deeply, tending instead to stay at the surface of the wood.

2. The second method is to use a wash coat or *stain controller* (widely available and also known as *wood conditioner*) before applying the stain. This liquid is absorbed into the wood fibers, sealing the surface of the wood and preventing the stain from penetrating unevenly. Match the type of controller to the stain you're using. Oil-based controllers work with oil-based stains, while water-based controllers work with water-based stains. Alternatively, you can use a thin coat of finish, either shellac, lacquer or varnish (called a wash coat) for just about any stain. Cut the finish 50:50 with its thinner to use it as a stain controller. Thinned shellac is very popular for wash coats, as it dries in about an hour and works with any stain except alcohol-based dyes. For these, use commercial oil-based controller.

Typically, oil-based controllers are applied generously to the wood surface, the excess is wiped off after 15 minutes, then the stain is applied. When shellac- and lacquer-based controllers are used, they should dry for at least one hour before applying the stain. The stain should not be alcohol- or lacquer-based, though, since they will dissolve the shellac- or lacquer-based sealer. No controller is 100% effective, however, so it's imperative that you practice staining on a cutoff piece first. In particularly nasty blotching cases, use both techniques (stain controller followed by a gel stain).

3. The third (and easiest) option for preventing blotching is to not use a stain at all and let the wood develop a color on its own.

Stain controllers

Stain controllers, sold under a variety of product names, are actually thinned finishes intended to minimize the blotching effects of stain on raw wood. Apply stain controller first, then stain the wood while the controller is still wet.

EFFECT OF STAIN CONTROLLERS

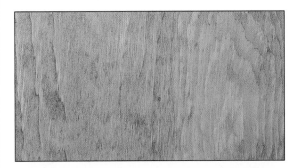

Liquid stain applied over untreated pine veneer looks blotchy and dark. Blotchiness is the result of uneven stain penetration on woods that lack an even surface grain density.

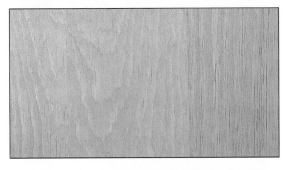

Liquid stain applied over pine veneer treated with a wash coat of stain controller has more even color penetration and is lighter in tone.

Gel stain applied over untreated pine veneer also provides more even color penetration, since gel stains do not penetrate wood surfaces as deeply as liquid stains.

HOW TO APPLY PIGMENT STAIN

1 To apply pigment stain, first mix it thoroughly to suspend the pigment particles. Be sure your project surface is clean and dry with no traces of glue (glue will not absorb stain). Wipe stain over the entire surface with a lint-free cloth, or apply it with a brush.

2 Allow the stain to penetrate into the wood for a minute or two (see the instructions on the container), then wipe away the excess. For a darker wood tone, you can try repeating the application, but pigment stains tend not to be cumulative so your best bet is to repeat with new, darker colored stain.

HOW TO APPLY DYE STAIN

1 Apply a generous amount of the dye stain to a lint-free cloth and brush it evenly onto the wood. Work quickly: dye stains tend to evaporate fast, which can cause ridges of darker color in the overlapping areas.

2 Switch to a clean rag and wipe off the excess stain before it dries. If you are mixing your own stain and you feel the color is too light, add pigment to the stain and reapply. If the color is too dark, wipe it down with stain solvent.

Filling wood pores & grain

All wood has vessels that conduct sap to the leaves when the tree is alive. When the tree is cut into lumber, these vessels are sliced open, revealing channels in the wood that look like drinking straws that have been cut open lengthwise. These are called *pores,* and what you do with these during finishing will determine the overall appearance of your project. On some hardwoods like oak, ash, mahogany and walnut, these pores are deep and visible after a finish is applied. If you want a glass-smooth finished surface, the pores need to be filled before applying finish. This is accomplished either with the finish itself or with paste wood filler (also called "grain filler").

If you do not fill the wood pores, they will be visible when viewed at certain angles—this is called an *open-pore finish.* You do not have to fill the pores. Open-pored finishes have a more natural, but less elegant, look that many woodworkers prefer.

It's possible to fill the pores with certain thick finishes, like varnish, but it's time-consuming. A better and more efficient product to use is paste wood filler. It's available in water-based or oil-based, and may

Apply paste wood filler if you want to create a smooth finish on your project without the pores showing through. Spread the filler over project surfaces with a brush and remove the excess with a scraper. Depending on the product, you can fill pores before or after staining.

be natural or colored. Natural is used in situations where you want to downplay the pores or have them match the surrounding color of the wood (it's an off-white color). Colored fillers are made with pigment and they're used to color the pores as well as the wood.

Application of a paste wood filler depends on the type. Water-based filler is best applied to the bare wood, allowed to dry, then sanded off. It can then be colored with non-grain-raising dye stains. Oil-based filler can be applied before or after staining but once applied, it cannot be stained.

THE EFFECT OF WOOD FILLERS ON GRAIN COLOR

No filler: This sample of mahogany plywood was simply stained and topcoated with varnish. No wood filler was used. Depending on how porous the wood is, pores may show through as dimples in the finish.

"Natural" filler: When wood pores are filled with "natural" tinted wood filler, the effect lightens the wood tone overall and evens out the contrast between porous areas and the surrounding flat grain.

Dark filler: Dark wood filler accentuates the wood pores and creates a contrast quite different from the unfilled sample at the far left. Dark wood fillers are best suited for darker woods like walnut, cherry or oak.

1 Water-based wood filler is applied to bare or stripped wood, prior to the stain and finish. Brush the filler product onto the wood with a stiff-bristle brush, working it into the wood pores with the brush.

2 Immediately remove the excess filler from the wood surface with a rubber squeegee or a piece of stiff cardboard (non-corrugated works better). Have a receptacle handy to dispose of the excess. Let the remaining filler dry to a dull haze—usually, from one to three hours.

3 Lightly sand the surface with 220-grit sandpaper. The goal is to remove the filler and residue from the wood surface, but leave it in the pores and, if you're so inclined, the wood grain. Let the filler dry for at least a day before wiping with a tack cloth and applying dye stain and/or finish.

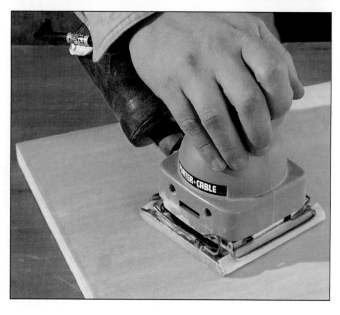

Applying water-based filler. To use a water-based filler, pick either the color that you want to use, or translucent if you want a clear filler. Apply it with a brush, remove the excess with a rubber squeegee or piece of cardboard, then let it dry. Using 220-grit sandpaper, sand the excess filler until the wood surface is clean, but the pores are still filled with filler. Let the filler dry for at least one day. While the surface may look chalky at first, the chalkiness disappears as soon as you apply finish or an alcohol-based dye stain. Any finish can be applied over a water-based filler.

Oil-based filler. Many professionals prefer oil-based paste wood filler. It allows you to stain the wood first to the color you want, seal the stain with a sealer coat of finish (shellac or varnish cut 50:50 with thinner is fine) and then let it dry. After lightly sanding with 400-grit sandpaper, apply the colored filler you want. Choose dark filler to highlight the pores or a lighter color that will blend in with the color of the flat grain in between the pores. On unstained, light woods like ash, use natural. You can also apply the filler to bare wood. Either way, application is the same.

Applying oil-based filler. Brush the filler onto the surface, then immediately remove as much of the excess as you can with a rubber squeegee. Wait until the filler hazes over (usually 15 minutes). Then, using a piece of burlap, terry cloth or cotton, wipe the excess filler off, working across the grain. When the wood is clean (filler should remain in the pores), let the filler dry for at least two days, and longer if it's cold. Lightly sand the dried filler with 400-grit paper before applying clear finish. Shellac, varnish and lacquer can be applied over an oil-based filler, but some water-based finishes may have adhesion problems. If in doubt, seal the filler in with a coat of de-waxed shellac.

How to apply oil-based filler

1 Oil-based filler is applied after the wood is stained, not before, making it a more popular product than water-based filler with many experienced wood finishers. Seal the stained wood surface with wood conditioner or a seal coat (See page 135). Thinned shellac is being applied as a seal coat in the photo above.

2 Brush a heavy coat of filler onto the dried, sealed surface with a relatively stiff brush. Work the filler into the wood pores and grain—a twisting motion helps get the filler all the way into the lower areas.

3 Scrape the excess filler from the wood surface with a rubber squeegee or stiff cardboard. Wait for about 15 minutes until the filler hazes over.

4 Wipe the filler residue from the wood surface with rough fabric, such as burlap. For best results, work across the grain. Do not overwork the surface. You want the filler to remain in the pores. Wait at least two days before applying finish.

Applying glazes

A glaze is a thin coat of color that is applied between coats of finish. It can be dye-based or pigment-based, but most are pigment-based. Glazes are very similar to pigment stains. In fact, pigment stains can be used as glazes but generally glazes dry more slowly and are thicker. The main uses for glaze are:

- To alter the hue or value.
- To highlight pore structure.
- To add richness and depth.
- To highlight grain.
- To imitate wood grain or other effects, such as aging.

Glazes are applied over a coat of finish by spray, brush or with a rag. Then they are either wiped off clean, leaving a thin coat of glaze behind, or they are manipulated by hand with various tools to create certain effects before they set up and start to dry. They are available in oil- or water-based versions.

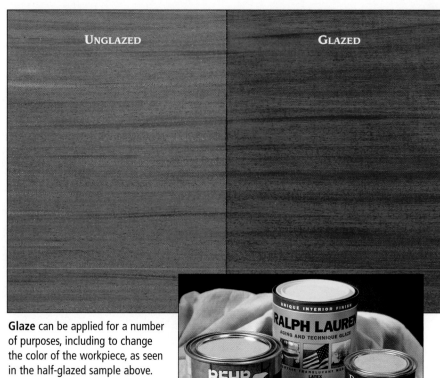

Glaze can be applied for a number of purposes, including to change the color of the workpiece, as seen in the half-glazed sample above. They are available in various forms. You can buy the glaze in the color you want or make it from a pre-mixed base that is uncolored. You can also make your own glazes from various raw materials.

SAMPLE GLAZING EFFECTS

Artificial aging of a newer finish is a very common glazing purpose. In the sample above, a freshly finished, but very new-looking, panel door was glazed with dark gel stain. The stain was simply wiped into the crevices where it would naturally collect, then feathered back into the field area with a rag. Finish was applied over the glazing and stain.

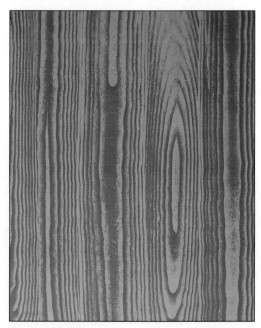

Faux wood graining is generally done using glazes and a special wood graining tool (available at most paint supply stores). A base coat of paint (satin or gloss) is applied to the surface to establish the background color. Then, a darker-toned glazing product is applied over the paint and worked with the graining tool to create texture and pattern.

Finishing wood

The wood finish, sometimes called the topcoat, is critical to the long-term durability of any furnishing, and also has a major impact on the general appearance. It should be smooth, evenly applied and of adequate thickness to form a contiguous layer of protection. It can be low-gloss, semi-gloss (satin) or high in gloss, depending mostly on personal preference.

Each of the hundreds of finishing products on the market today can be grouped into a manageable category in accordance with its general working qualities, degree of protection and basic constitution. These groups are waxes, oils, varnishes, shellac, lacquer and water-based finishes. Different finishes have varying degrees of protection, durability, ease of application, repairability and aesthetic appeal. Unfortunately there is no finish that excels in all of these categories. So choosing a finish is mostly about making trade-offs: a finish that excels in one category may not be a good choice in another.

When choosing a finish, consider the following:

• How will the item be used? Is it subjected to a lot of exposure to moisture, solvents, food, or general abuse? Or will it be primarily a display piece?

• What is your skill level?

• What is the condition of the work area where the finish will be applied? Does it stay clean and is it heated, dry and well ventilated?

• What do you want the wood to look like? Do you prefer an "in the wood" natural look, or a thicker finish that accentuates depth?

• Will you be filling the pores?

• What color, if any, do you want the finish to impart to the wood?

• Is yellowing an issue? Do you want to minimize changes in color as the wood ages?

(Continued on page 144)

Lacquer

The term *lacquer* generally means a fast-drying glossy, hard finish based upon flammable solvents. It is still considered by many professionals to be the best all-around finish for wood, as it is fast-drying, it imparts depth and richness, it has moderate to excellent durability (depending on the type used) and it rubs out well. Nitrocellulose lacquers are the most common lacquer you will find and if the label on the can says lacquer—it's this type. It's probably one of the hardest finishes for beginners and amateurs to work with, as it's best applied with spray equipment and is difficult to brush on. A good solution for getting the benefits of lacquer, but avoiding the application challenges, is to use spray lacquer in aerosol-can form. They are easy to apply, but can get expensive for large projects.

True oils

Oil is a word that's used a lot in finishing. Right away, we need to make a distinction between oils that do not dry or form a solid when exposed to air (called *non-drying oils*) and ones that do form a solid when exposed to air (called *drying oils*). An example of a non-drying oil is mineral oil. The two drying oils used in finishing are boiled linseed oil and tung oil. Though other drying oils have been used, these two are easily available and inexpensive. In an effort to distinguish these two products from other products hyped as oil finishes, we call these *true oils*.

Oils do not dry as hard as other finishes, and can even settle into a soft, gummy state if you try to build them up to a thick finish. On the other hand, they are easy to apply, they repair easily and they add depth and luster to wood. These are always sold under names like boiled linseed oil or pure tung oil. Tung oil is a tad bit more water-resistant, lighter in color, and it yellows less than linseed oil.

NOTE: Water-based products (like the "Polycrylic" below) technically aren't varnish but have similar properties. See page 145.

Varnish

Varnish is an inexact word, It has meant different things throughout history and remains confusing today. But in general usage, *varnish* normally refers to finishes that are made from hard, tough and durable synthetic resins like alkyd, phenolic and urethane. These resins are heated to react chemically with oils. The resulting product is much more durable than oil alone.

There are two general groupings of varnish: "long oil varnishes" that have a high percentage of oil in the finish, and "short oil varnishes" with a lower percentage of oil. Long oil varnishes are also known as marine varnishes, spar varnishes or just plain exterior varnishes. They are soft and flexible. Short oil varnishes are for interior use and dry to a harder, less elastic film. Varnishes are typically applied with a brush, although thinned varnishes and gel versions can be wiped on.

Oil/varnish blends

Oil/varnish blends have some of the qualities of true oils (they can be wiped on easily, for example) but pick up some of the enhanced protective qualities of varnish. Unlike varnish, which is a product formed from the chemical reaction between oil and resin, think of these products as varnish thinned with a lot of oil. The oil reduces the gloss, and reduces some of the protective qualities. *Watco,* Danish oil, teak oil, Nordic oils, and a host of the other finishes sold as oil finishes fall into this category.

Many finishers prefer to make their own oil/varnish blends so they know exactly what's in it. A good general recipe follows the rule of thirds: ⅓ varnish (pick your favorite), ⅓ oil (linseed or tung) and ⅓ mineral sprits. Since the oil increases drying time, many finishers prefer to cut back on the amount of oil. Another recipe calls for one cup varnish, one cup naphtha and ⅓ cup linseed oil. You can always substitute mineral spirits for the naphtha to slow down the open time. Add Japan drier (an additive to speed up the dry time) after application. Typically, an ounce or two per gallon is added, though you should read the instructions on the can.

Shellac

While most people think of shellac as a liquid that you buy in a paint store, it's really a natural resin that's derived from the secretions of the Lac bug—an insect that feeds off trees indigenous to India and Thailand. The secretion is in the form of cocoons that are gathered from the trees and eventually refined into dry flakes. The flakes are dissolved in alcohol to create the liquid shellac.

Shellac is available in dry flake form. When blended with denatured alcohol, shellac made with de-waxed flakes has a shelf life of six months or so. Pre-mixed shellac generally contains wax and has a shelf life of up to three years, manufacturers claim. With shellac, the fresher the solution the better it will work. Its resistance to water and ability to dry to a hard film both diminish as it ages.

Pre-mixed shellac is available in orange (amber) and clear (which is shellac that's been bleached). Shellac flakes are available in a wider variety of colors and wax contents than the pre-mixed variety. Wax decreases the resistance of shellac to water and prevents some finishes from bonding to it.

Shellac can be wiped on or applied with a brush, but either way the best results occur when you apply thin coats. Because the finish dries rapidly, two or three coats can be applied in a day. When dissolving flakes for wiping or brushing, use a "two-pound cut." Technically, this refers

to a ratio of two pounds of shellac dissolved in one gallon of alcohol, but since this creates much more material than you'll need for most projects, reduce the recipe. A more manageable quantity is created by dissolving four ounces, by weight, of dry shellac in one pint (16 ounces) of denatured alcohol. The pre-mixed shellac is typically blended as a three-pound cut. It can (and usually should) be reduced to a two-pound cut by thinning it with denatured alcohol at a rate of one pint alcohol per quart of premixed shellac.

Sand between coats of finish with 320- or 400-grit sandpaper to smooth out wood grain that may have been raised by the moisture in the product (especially if using a water-based finish) and to eliminate slight imperfections in the finish. Then wipe the surface thoroughly with a tack cloth to remove all traces of grit before recoating with finish.

Condition the brush before applying finish by dipping the bristles all the way up to the ferrule (the metal band) in the thinner for the finish you'll be using. Use water for water-based finishes, mineral spirits for oil-based var-nishes and alcohol for shellac. Remove excess thinner from the bristles with a rag. Condition-ing makes the brush easier to clean later.

Sanding sealer accomplishes just what its name implies: it seals wood fibers, oils and stains to prepare a sur-face for sanding. Pre-mixed sanding sealers, de-waxed shellac or a mixture of equal parts varnish and mineral spir-its (above photo) all make good sealer coats. Apply sanding sealer with a brush (right photo) just as you would other brushed finishes.

• Will you rub the finish out to the sheen you like? Or are you depending on the inherent qualities of the finish to establish the sheen?

• Are you sensitive to certain solvents? Is flammability an issue for you? Are you concerned about the environmental impact of cer-tain finishes?

Finish features

Durability. Durability is essen-tially a measure of a product's resistance to water, chemicals and solvents (like alkaline cleaners and acidic foods), heat and scratches. Waxes, oils, shellac, lacquer and some water-based finishes can be damaged if exposed to water long enough. Shellac is not resistant to alkalis, like ammonia, or to alco-hol. Most of these products will scratch easily, but they do polish well (that's the flip side of scratch resistance).

Varnish, some water-based fin-ishes and polyurethane are gener-ally the most durable wood finishing products.

Ease of application. Your degree of skill, the environment you have to work in and the tools you have access to play a part in choosing the best finish. If you're a beginner, a wipe-on, wipe-off finish like Dan-ish oil is far easier to apply than brushing shellac. If the environ-ment you have to work in is cold, or there's always sanding dust in the air, the fast-drying finishes are a good bet. Shellac and lacquer are the least temperamental when it comes to cold temperatures, and can be modified with additives (retarder) for hot and humid condi-tions. Oils and oil-based products dry slowly in cold temperatures and humid conditions, and dust is always a problem as they remain tacky for a long time, giving dust the opportunity to become embed-ded in the surface.

Aesthetics. This category has to do with how you want the wood to look. Do you want a natural finish or an elegant, deep, glass-smooth

(Continued on page 146)

Water-based finishes

Water-based finishes are most often water-based lacquer and water-based polyurethane, but other resins are sometimes used as noted below. Technically, you can make a water-based anything, varnish and shellac included, but since there are very few they do not merit separate classification.

Water-based finishes are made of similar components as other finishes, most notably urethane, alkyd and acrylic, but the flammable and polluting solvents are partially replaced with water. The chemistry involved in doing this is a little complex because none of these resins have a natural affinity for water unless they are chemically modified or forced to combine with water in a chemical mixture called an emulsion.

Water-based finishes will raise wood grain. There are several ways to deal with this:

- Deliberately raise the grain by wiping the wood with distilled water, then re-sand it with the last grit in your sanding sequence (like 220). The grain will raise less when a finish is applied.
- Seal the wood with a coat of de-waxed shellac.
- Seal the wood with several coats of water-based finish, then sand it with 400-grit sandpaper until it's smooth. Use silicon carbide, wet/dry sandpaper.

Strain water-based finishes through a medium mesh or paper filter to remove bits of dried finish that may be present in the can. It's a good idea to strain out only as much finish as you plan to use. Pour what you don't use through a clean strainer back into the original can.

Raise the grain first, before staining, with distilled water. Wipe project surfaces down using a sponge or rag dampened with distilled water. Allow the wood to dry. Then, sand with 220-grit paper. By deliberately raising the grain and knocking it off, you'll reduce the amount of grain-raising produced by the first finish coat.

Apply a sealer coat of de-waxed shellac. Shellac will seal the wood pores and minimize water absorption. Lightly sand the sealer once it dries to smooth the surface, then apply the finish.

finish that accentuates depth and luster? Is the color of the finish (many varnishes and shellacs impart an amber or light-orange tone) a problem, and will yellowing of the finish be a problem later? Traditionally, woodworkers have turned to the oils (tung and linseed), wax, or oil-varnish blends for a natural finish. However, any finish can be used for this effect. As long as you don't build up the finish beyond several coats, shellac, lacquer, and varnish can all be used for natural-looking finishes. Hard, film-forming finishes like shellac, lacquer or varnish have to be used if you're going for a filled-pore, deep, lustrous finish.

The color and the penetration of the finish itself may be an issue. Orange shellac or varnish both may have a color that's too dark for woods you want to keep as light as possible. As a rule, oils and oil-based varnishes deepen color of the wood and increase luster the most, followed by solvent-based lacquers and shellac. Water-based polyurethane or acrylic finishes tend to lie on the surface and do not penetrate, which has the effect of keeping the wood lighter.

The "plastic" look that's sometimes ascribed to finishes like polyurethane and varnish has to do more with incorrect application of these finishes than the finishes themselves. On open-pored woods, application of thick varnishes and lacquers results in a "soupy" look to the pores, a result of the finish bridging the pore rather than flowing into it. Proper application of these finishes, including thinning, results in a more attractive look. A good formula for applying oil-based polyurethane is to thin the finish 50% and wipe it on.

Yellowing of the finish is a problem over white and painted finishes (yellowed lacquer over a blue paint will turn it green) or if your intentions are to retain the natural color of the wood as much as possible. Yellowing is caused by the finish reacting to light and is most noticeable with solvent lacquer and oil-based varnishes and polyurethane. Acrylic-based finishes, both water and solvent-based, are the best choice for non-yellowing finishes.

Safety/environmental issues. Solvent-based finishes like varnish and lacquer contain organic solvents, which are flammable and hazardous both to you and the environment. If this is a problem for you, use a water-based finish to eliminate the fire problem and mitigate the environmental and health hazards. Shellac is also a good alternative. The solvent for shellac, ethyl alcohol, is distilled from corn. For most people, the odor isn't objectionable, although it is flammable.

All finishes are non-toxic when fully cured, despite what you may have read or heard. Once the solvents are evaporated, the cured film is safe enough for contact with food. This does not mean that the finish itself is safe to gobble up. It means that additives such as driers or plasticizers are encapsulated enough so that they do not migrate to your food.

1 After conditioning the brush, dip it into the finish product so the bristles are submerged no more than halfway.

Brushing on a finish

Before brushing, make sure the brush is clean by whacking it against your palm or the edge of a table to dislodge any dirt or debris. Then "condition" the brush by dipping it all the way up to the ferrule in the thinner for the finish you'll be using (See page 144). Use water for water-based finishes, mineral spirits for oil-based varnishes and alcohol for shellac. After straining the finish into a smaller container through a medium mesh strainer to remove any bits of debris or dried finish, dip the brush into the finish halfway up (never farther). Bring the brush out of the liquid and press it against the side of the can to remove excess finish. Never scrape it across the lip of the can. This can cause air bubbles in the finish.

For oil-based and alcohol-based finishes, use a natural bristle brush of decent quality (See page 130). For water-based finishes, a synthetic-bristle brush will do the job.

When brushing on a finish, the most common mistake beginners make is to overwork the material in an effort to get it even and to remove air bubbles. Once the finish is laid down, let it be.

2 Gently wipe the broad edges of the brush on the side of the container (not against the lip) to press our excess material.

3 Apply the finish to the workpiece, starting at an end. Begin brushing a couple of inches in from the end, working toward the edge. Use smooth, light strokes.

Always brush toward the edge

4 Work from the end where you started and toward the opposite end (on flat surfaces), overlapping the brush strokes. Do not overwork the finish. If air bubbles develop, leave them be and they'll likely disappear as the finish dries. Avoid ridges in the overlap area.

5 Once the entire surface is coated, it's okay to "tip-off" the finish by very lightly almost "tickling" it with the dry tip of the brush. Let the finish dry as recommended, sand very lightly to knock down finish defects, then recoat. Apply at least three thin coats.

Correcting Finishing Problems

Even professionals cannot avoid occasional problems in the finish. If caught in time, they are usually correctable. The most common are "fish-eyes," bubbles and drips.

Fish-eyes. When wood is stripped, waxes and silicone from polishes can remain in the wood. When finishes other than shellac are applied, small dome-like craters form in the finish. These are called "fish-eyes." The best time to prevent them is prior to applying the finish. Wax can be removed by wiping refinished items several times with naphtha or mineral spirits, but silicone is impossible to completely remove. It has a rather tenacious ability to remain in pores or small cracks in wood, and the solvents rarely can pull it out. If you see fish-eyes, immediately wipe off your finishing product (oil-based stains will fish-eye as well) and wash the piece down with mineral spirits or naphtha. Then scrub it well with TSP or a TSP substitute and fine synthetic steel wool. Then apply a freshly made (less than six months old) coat of two-pound, de-waxed shellac. The thinner for shellac (alcohol) doesn't react to silicone the way that other finish solvents do, so the shellac lays over the silicone, isolating it. When the shellac is dry, you can apply any finish you wish over the shellac. When using solvent lacquer over a shellac sealer, it's possible to dissolve the shellac with too wet a coat, so you should apply lighter coats. Re-emergence of silicone after cleaning and sealing with shellac is such a problem with solvent lacquer that most production and professional finishers add a silicone-based additive to the lacquer. This is the best solution for these folks, but additives aren't always easily available for finishes other than lacquer. In these cases, thorough washing as described above followed by de-waxed shellac is the best remedy.

Bubbles. Bubbles occur only with varnish and polyurethane and with some water-based products. They do not occur with shellac, lacquer or oils. The primary culprits that cause bubbles are incorrect brush choice and applying the finish in layers that are too thick. To avoid bubbling, thin the finish first: just an ounce or two per pint of finish to start. If that doesn't work, try switching to a different brush. If you still get bubbles, make sure that the finish, the project and the room temperature are all 65° or warmer. If all else fails, try a different finish.

Drips. Drips are easy to fix. If you get one, wipe it immediately and re-brush the area. If you miss it and it's partially dry, leave it alone and when it's dry, slice it off with a razor blade or sharp chisel. Starting about 3 in. from an edge, brush the finish toward the edge and off. If you start right at the edge, you'll get a very large drip. Then, come back immediately to where you started, and continue the brush stroke to the other end. As the brush dries out, replenish it.

Wiping on a finish

Any finish can be wiped onto a piece of furniture, but the easiest products to wipe are varnish and oil finishes. Of the two, oil finishes are easier than varnish, because the finish is simply applied to the wood, allowed to sit for a while, then wiped off. Varnishes are a little more difficult to wipe on, but

HOW TO WIPE ON SHELLAC

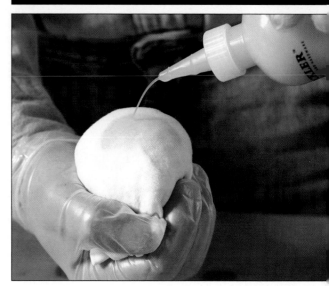

1 Make a shellac pad by wadding up a piece of clean, lint-free cloth then wrapping the wadded cloth in another clean cloth. Make sure the exposed surface of the cloth that you'll be wiping with is free of wrinkles or creases. Fill a squirt bottle with shellac and squirt a generous amount onto the pad.

HOW TO WIPE ON VARNISH

1 Varnish is easy to wipe on. Fold up a non-textured paper towel, dip it into a bowl of thinned varnish, and start. It is forgiving, so feel free to use whatever wiping strategy you're comfortable with.

because they dry harder than oil, they provide greater protection. Shellac also may be applied by wiping if a proper "shellac pad" is used (See below).

To wipe varnish or polyurethane, use a product made specifically for wiping, or just make your own by thinning your favorite varnish or polyurethane 50:50 with mineral spirits or naphtha (naphtha dries faster).

Using a piece of lint-free cloth or a non-textured paper towel (See page 130), wipe the varnish on in smooth, even strokes. Overlap each stroke by about an inch. Work with a light illuminating the back of the piece so you can see if you've missed a spot and correct it immediately. Once the finish is down, do not mess with it. You'll only make it worse.

2 Wipe the shellac onto the furniture surfaces in long, sweeping, back-and-forth passes. Begin at one end and work in a continuous pass to the other end. Do not press down too hard: let the shellac "flow" off the pad.

3 As you near edges, begin raising the pad so it is barely contacting the surface when it passes over the edge. Coat the entire surface as evenly as you can, avoid ridges and overworking the finish. Sand lightly when dry, wipe clean with a tack cloth, then apply additional coats of shellac.

2 After the surfaces have been coated and allowed to dry, gently wipe them down with 0000 steel wool. Wipe with a tack cloth, then apply the next coat.

3 Apply the final coat (you should apply at least three) with a lamp positioned to cast glancing light across the surface. This makes it easier to spot any trouble areas as you work.

Spraying on a finish

Spraying on a finish has always been considered an advanced finish application technique. But advances in spray equipment technology (especially the HVLP sprayer) and finish products themselves have made spraying a legitimate option even for the casual do-it-yourselfer. This is good news, since no other finish application method can rival the speed, uniformity and ease of a correctly applied, sprayed finish. Be aware, however, that a professional-looking sprayed finish will have a "commercial" quality that may not be appropriate on older pieces and antiques, where the minor fluctuations and imperfections in the finish contribute to the overall feeling of the piece.

Spraying basics. There are several steps to follow for using any spray system.

• You thin the material to be sprayed so that your particular setup can handle it.

• You match the proper nozzle/valve combination to the finish you're spraying.

• You adjust the controls on the gun and compressor (if possible) for optimum spraying efficiency and finish quality.

• You use proper techniques for spraying.

• The gun must be properly cleaned and maintained after using.

Thinning. Most finishes are too thick to be sprayed, so you'll need to thin the material with the appropriate solvent. Some materials need a lot of solvent (as much as 50%) to be adequately atomized. Others require very little or none at all. Most HVLP turbine systems sold to novice finishers come with a chart and a device called a viscosity drip cup for determining finish viscosity (See next page). Adding thinner will solve problems like *orange peel:* a pebbly look to the finish after it's dry.

Needle/Nozzle. These parts are provided with most systems and are matched to the type of finish being sprayed. Generally, smaller aperture fluid nozzles are used with clear lacquers, while larger aperture ones are used with oil varnishes and paints.

Gun controls. Most quality guns have two controls to control the rate (amount) at which the finish is released and the amount of air that's released with it. Controlling the air at the gun only affects the pattern of spray—from small and round to a wide, fan-shaped pattern. Increasing the amount of air from the air source will improve atomization of the finish, but sometimes at the

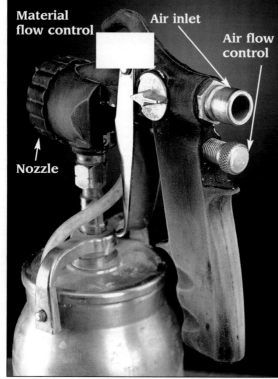

Material flow control · Air inlet · Air flow control · Nozzle

Get to know your spray gun. The material flow control regulates the amount of finish that is sprayed. The nozzle is adjusted to change the spray pattern. The air flow control adjusts air flow into the gun (some guns don't have this feature).

HVLP sprayers (High Volume/Low Pressure) deliver finish materials in a very efficient spray that's easy to control. Typically, they have their own internal turbine system to generate air pressure. As they have become more popular, the prices have come down dramatically, positioning them within reach of most people's budget.

expense of transfer efficiency. Most turbine systems have a set flow of air that can't be regulated, while compressor drive systems can be regulated at the compressor or with a valve installed near the gun. Some guns do not have a pattern control knob at the back of the gun. Instead, the pattern is controlled by the air cap.

Proper technique. The gun is always held at a 90° angle to the work and usually 6 to 10 in. away. HVLP guns are generally held closer. The gun should be held in a "locked" position with your arm so that you avoid swinging the gun in an arc—this will change the dis-

Compressor-driven spray guns are relatively inexpensive attachments you can buy for your air compressor. For the beginner, they're a little harder to handle than HVLP sprayers, and they also tend to produce considerably more overspray. Nevertheless, they can certainly be effective tools for spraying a finish if you're willing to spend some time getting the feel of them. They require anywhere from 2 to 8 cubic feet per minute (CFM) of air and operate best at 90 to 120 pounds per square inch (psi) of pressure.

Use a viscosity cup to time the flow rate of the finishing material, thinning as needed to match the specific flow rate for your paint sprayer. Most spraying equipment will come with charts that indicate the preferred viscosity level for various types of material.

1 Thin the finish and set up the gun with the best needle-nozzle settings for the task. When possible, the surface being finished should be horizontal to minimize runs. Start spraying at the edges of flat workpieces so you don't cover the flat surfaces with overspray after they've already been finished. Hold the gun about 8 in. away from the work and move it in a steady plane at a rate of 10 to 12 in. per second.

2 Begin finishing flat surfaces near the edge. Work slowly enough to get the surface good and wet, but not so wet that it starts to puddle. As with any finish application technique, the best results are created by several thin coats.

tance between the gun and the workpiece. The trigger is depressed before you hit the edge of the piece and released after you leave it.

When spraying a flat surface, start at the edge closest to you and spray wet coats of finish away from you, overlapping each pass by about half. Each pass should make the wood look wet, but don't go too slow, or you'll puddle the finish. When spraying complicated pieces, like a chair, it's best to spray the least visible areas first (like the undersides and stretchers) and then work toward the most visible (the seat and tops of the arms). It's also advisable to use a lazy-susan type turntable bearing with a piece of plywood on it so you can turn the piece easily as you spray it.

The proper adjustments and technique will result in a smooth, even coat of fin-

ish after it's dry. Keep in mind that water-based finishes may look terrible until they dry for at least eight hours. Solvent-based finishes should look pretty good after about an hour.

Using a spray gun for the first time

If you've never used spray equipment before, you can practice a bit and play with the controls by spraying plain water or solvent through the gun. Fill up the cup and turn all the controls on the back of the gun clockwise to close them off. Hold the gun so you have light behind it and start opening the fluid rate knob. A round, fine mist of water should start to appear. As you turn the knob more, a denser spray pattern will start to appear. Experiment with opening and closing the knob until you get the feel of it.

Next, open the air control knob and observe how the pattern gets wider or fuller as you open it. If the gun doesn't have this adjustment, turn the air cap to change the spray pattern. Once you have the feel of the controls and where

they should be set, try spraying water on a piece of cardboard to get the feel for how far to hold the gun from the surface and how fast to move it (in most cases, about 10 to 12 in. per second).

Now, try using real finish in the gun. Fill it up with thinned finish and, holding the gun up so that you can see the spray from the side, depress the trigger. You should see a fine mist of finish spray out from the gun. If not, try adding more thinner to the finish or switch to a different nozzle/needle combo. Or, increase the air supply from the air source (if you can). When you get it right, begin spraying a flat piece of scrap wood. Experiment with the adjustments until you see a full, wet swath of finish when you hold the gun 8 in. from the wood.

3 Work your way across the workpiece in straight passes, overlapping each swath by about half. Whenever possible, move the gun farther away from your body as you proceed. Always keep the nozzle at a 90° angle to the wood surface.

4 As each surface is completed, adjust your position or the position of the workpiece and immediately apply a second pass in swaths that are perpendicular to the first pass. Let the finish dry, sand it lightly and wipe it clean, then apply additional coats. Clean the nozzle after each coat and the rest of the equipment when the project is done.

Cleaning spray equipment

Spray equipment requires thorough cleaning after each use. Start cleaning by pouring some solvent into the container and running the gun. Spray the solvent onto a piece of cardboard and let the cardboard dry before discarding it. Then, disassemble the spray gun nozzle and assembly, and clean the individual parts using the solvent recommended for the finishing material used: usually mineral spirits (oil-based), water (latex), or lacquer thinner (lacquer). Make sure all parts are thoroughly clean and dry before storing them.

Rubbing a finish to a flat sheen involves sanding the surface with 600-grit silicon-carbide sandpaper, lubricated with mineral spirits. Sand edges and corners gently to avoid cutting through the finish.

Raise the finish to a satin luster by rubbing it with oil soap or thinned furniture paste wax and 0000 steel wool.

Switch to automotive rubbing compound, pumice powder or rottenstone and a soft cloth to rub the finish out to a gloss sheen.

Rubbing out a finish, waxing & polishing

The final coat of finish can be left alone, as is the case with satin finishes, or it can be "improved" by rubbing. This has the effect of removing bits of dust and debris, and also levels the finish and establishes the sheen you want. Only hard finishes can be rubbed out: oils and oil/varnish blends cannot be rubbed. The process is easier when the finish is hard, so let the finish cure at least a week for lacquers and shellac and two weeks for oil-based varnishes and polyurethane.

To rub out a finish, take a piece of 600 wet/dry silicon-carbide paper and sand the surface using mineral spirits or soapy water as a lubricant. Then, wipe off the residue and, using 0000 steel wool, rub the finish. Start with short, choppy strokes near the edges, then work the surface in long, even strokes. The effect of this rubbing will be a flat sheen.

To raise up the sheen (increase the gloss) a little, buff with steel wool and furniture paste wax thinned 50:50 with mineral spirits. Or, use an oil soap, like *Murphy's Oil Soap.* This will produce a satin gloss. To rub to high gloss, rub the finish with 4F pumice after dry-buffing with steel wool, then follow up with rottenstone, which is a polishing powder available at paint and hardware stores. You can substitute rubbing compounds from an automotive store for these two products if you wish.

Routine maintenance can be performed on finishes by a yearly re-waxing, or simply wiping down with mineral spirits or an emulsion polish (like *Pledge* or *Guardsman*) periodically to remove dirt. If the idea of commercial polish doesn't appeal to you, an effective cleaning solution can be made by mixing a capful of *Dawn* dishwashing detergent in a pint of warm water.

HOW TO APPLY A WAX FINISH

For added protection, wax the new finish. To apply the wax, wrap a golf-ball-sized lump with a 10-in.-square piece of cheesecloth (See inset photo) and rub the cheesecloth ball over the finish. The wax will seep through the cloth evenly as you put pressure on it. When the wax dries, buff off the haze.

Other useful routine maintenance and repair methods include:

• Scratches can be removed by the steel-wooling process as described above for rubbing out. If they are deep, fill the scratch with topcoat finish, wet-sand and apply finish to blend it in (See pages 72 to 83).

• Dents and gouges are repaired easily using wax filler sticks, which are sold in a range of wood tone colors. Apply the color closest to the general color of the wood or mix several colors to get a better match. See pages 76 to 78.

• To clean a finish, wipe it first with mineral spirits and 0000 steel wool, followed by a cleaning with warm water and dish soap. Apply a couple of coats of furniture paste wax. See pages 80 to 81.

• General dings, dents and areas of missing color can be easily fixed with a waxing or application of a dark colored polish (sometimes called "scratch remover"). Apply the polish with a soft cloth and then wipe the excess off with a clean cloth. See pages 72 to 75.

Regularly clean and polish furniture with mineral spirits, applied with a soft rag. If you prefer, use scented commercial furniture polish (emulsion type).

Painting furniture

Painted furniture is often underrated, with current preferences running toward retaining natural wood tones. But the fact is, there are some types of furniture, and some types of wood, that actually look better painted. The key, as with any finish, is to choose good finishing products and apply them carefully and correctly.

While latex-based paints are less toxic and easier to clean up than their oil-based counterparts, most furnituremakers still prefer oil-based products. Enamel oil-based paint dries to create a very hard protective surface. It's also easier to create a smooth finish with oil-based paints. Still, if you prefer working with latex paints, you can get reasonably good results as long as you use an enamel primer.

Woods with narrow, tight grain, such as birch and poplar, work best for painting. Pine is also a frequent choice for painted furniture: it takes the paint well, and you're not paying for wood with good figure just to cover it up with paint.

Supplies for painting furniture include: sandpaper; wood putty for filling voids, nail and screw holes, and wood defects; oil-based enamel paint; primer/sealer; a paint roller for broad surfaces; and sponge brushes for smooth paint application.

How to paint furniture

1 Fill nail holes or screw holes, knots and other surface defects with paintable wood filler putty. Apply the putty so its surface is slightly higher than the surrounding wood surface when dry.

2 Sand the filled areas so they're smooth and level with the surrounding wood. For most projects, use 100- or 150-grit sandpaper to remove the excess material, then sand with 180-grit sandpaper to remove rough spots and sanding marks. Wipe the surface thoroughly with a damp rag or a tack cloth.

3 Apply a thin coat of primer/sealer. Primer/sealer helps the paint bond more evenly, and forms a protective layer to prevent agents within the wood from seeping out and causing stains in the painted surface. It's not critical, but generally you should use oil-based primer with oil-based paint. NOTE: Instead of commercial primer/sealer, some woodworkers prefer to use a mixture of thinned orange shellac and boiled linseed oil for the primer coat.

4 Scuff the primed surface lightly with 180- or 220-grit sandpaper after the primer dries. This creates "tooth" on the surface so the paint will bond better. Be sure to wipe the primed surface with a tack cloth or damp rag before applying the first coat of paint.

5 Apply a thin, even coat of enamel oil-based paint to all surfaces. The most common mistake made when painting is to apply layers that are too thick. An overly heavy coat of paint can sag and dry unevenly. If you can't see the primer coat at all through the first coat of paint, you've probably applied too much paint.

6 Apply the next coat. As a rule, let the first coat dry overnight no matter what the paint can tells you: a chief cause of paint failure is moisture trapped between coats. Apply additional coats, scuff-sanding lightly between coats. Three to four thin coats should yield a fine painted finish.

Index

Manufacturer's Reference (catalogs)

IASCO Industrial Arts Supply Co.
Casting supplies
1-888-919-0899
www.IASCO-TESCO.com

Klingspor's Sanding Catalogue
Sanding supplies, tools, finishing products
1-800-228-0000

Lee Valley Tools Ltd.
Tools, hardware
1-800-871-8158

The Renovator's Supply, Inc.
Hardware, moldings
1-800-659-2211

Rockler Woodworking & Hardware
Tools, hardware, glues, finishing products, moldings
1-800-260-9663
www.rockler.com

Van Dyke's Restorers
Tools, hardware, casting supplies, finishing products, moldings
1-800-558-1234
www.vandykes.com

Woodcraft
Tools, hardware, glues, finishing products, moldings
1-800-225-1153